Luba Gurdjieff

A Memoir with Recipes

Luba Gurdjieff

A Memoir with Recipes

Luba Gurdjieff Everitt

with

Marina C. Bear

SLG BOOKS

Berkeley-Hong Kong

Originally published in 1993 by Ten Speed Press

This edition published in 1997 by

SLG BOOKS
PO. Box 9465
Berkeley, CA 94709
Tel: 510-525-11345
Fax: 510-525-2632

Book and cover designs by Fifth Street Design

Printed by
Snow Lion Graphics
Berkeley/Hong Kong

Library of Congress Cataloging-in-Publication Data

Everitt, Luba Gurdjieff
   Luba Gurdjieff : a memoir with recipes / Luba Gurdjieff Everitt
with Marina C. Bear.
       p.   cm.
   Originally published: Berkeley, Calif. : Ten Speed Press, © 1993
   includes index.
   ISBN 0-943389-22-4 (trade paper)
   1. Everitt, Luba Gurdjieff. 2. Restauranteurs--England--London-
-Biography. 3. Luba's Bistro (Restaurant--History). 4. Gurdjieff,
Georges Ivanovitch, 1872-1949. 5. Cookery, Russian. I. Bear,
Marina C., 1941-   . II Title.
TX910.5.E83A3   1997
  647.94'092--dc21
   [b]   97-24599
                                                            CIP

Acknowledgements

Luba thanks her many friends and customers of the
Bistro over the years.

ॐ

Thanks also to John Bear and George Bennett, without
whose help this book would not have come to be.

Contents

Introduction

This is a simple book about the remarkable life of a thoroughly extraordinary woman. And this is how it came about.

We were planning a trip to England, my husband and I — a pilgrimage of sorts — and we asked an English friend for recommendations. "Avebury," he said. "The most geomantically perfect western village. And there are some people you might want to look up in the lowlands of Scotland. And Luba! Of course, you should stop to see Luba. Mr. Gurdjieff's niece, you know. Just tell her Reshad Feild said you should call."

Mr. Gurdjieff's niece! Whatever it took, that was a suggestion I was determined to follow up. I had met people who had known Gurdjieff after he had arrived in France in the 1920s. To this day, his powerful ideas continue to influence people interested in spiritual development. For more than twenty years I had been studying his ideas, wrestling with them, trying to live them. But to meet a relative — and a woman, at that; to see what a lifetime of contact with that discipline might produce was irresistible.

And so we went. Laden with flowers and teatime offerings, we knocked at the door of a tall, thin, white-painted row house that looked like dozens of others except for an exuberance of greenery spilling over a second-story balcony. As we climbed the narrow staircase, a voice rang down. "Welcome, welcome. Oh, such lovely flowers! Arthur, look! My favorites. And cakes — so many kinds. Why do you bring me all this rubbish? You think I can't feed you? Never mind, darlings. It's lovely. We'll eat it all."

To have tea with Luba is to be filled with food and stories, wonderful stories. On the way back to our hotel that evening, trying to remember everything, I found myself wondering what makes a person as exceptional as the one we'd just met. Luba sees everything with penetrating clarity and remains utterly positive. She combines the wisdom of more than seventy years with a vitality and intensity of someone half her age. In a time when youth is the only stage of life most people seem to think worth celebrating, she demonstrates the richness and intrinsic worth of a full life, fully lived. I kept thinking of people I wanted to introduce to her. There were too many. The seed of this book had been planted.

The question is intriguing: What makes someone like that? Heredity and environment certainly combined to give Luba Dmitrieevna Gurdjieff an unusual start. I found myself thinking in the rhythm of her speech, telling myself pieces of her story. Her family had fled the turmoil of revolutionary Russia for the refuge of her uncle's Institute for the Harmonious Development of Man at Fontainebleau, in France. There at the Prieuré, Luba was raised amid a constantly changing cast of seekers and students, artists, intellectuals and politicians who came to her uncle for guidance, drawn to him as a source of the eastern wisdom he interpreted for the west.

A childhood of hard work and extravagant play was interrupted for four long years as Luba struggled to overcome tuberculosis of the bone, but her singular vitality lightened the time spent in a sanitarium, and the visits of her uncle and family drew her back to health and her life at the Prieuré. Her education was in her uncle's hands, but it was at her mother's side, in the kitchens of the Prieuré, that she learned the secrets of the stove which were to earn her a place in London's heart.

It may be impossible for us to appreciate what it was like to live with a patriarch. The word has become synonymous with autocrat. The images surrounding it are oppressive, stunting, tyrannic. But at the Prieuré, Gurdjieff was a true patriarch, spiritual father to his students, provider and sustainer to his numerous relatives. Luba said that after he died, a steady stream of people appeared at her mother's door to pay their respects and offer condolences to the family. Some of them she knew, but the vast majority were people she had never seen before. All had been helped, spiritually and materially, throughout their lives by her uncle.

For Luba her uncle was a constant presence: "my Uncle." Life at the Prieuré shaped itself around him. The children struggled to stay in his good graces, hoping for a reward — perhaps a chance to go on one of his famous car trips. The adults who came to extract what they could from his teaching focused on his every word, every nuance of his behavior. Meanwhile, the family, missing from most of his followers' accounts of

Prieuré life, were the transparent laborers upon whom much of the château's functioning depended.

The Second World War saw the end of life at the Prieuré, and by 1950, Luba felt it was time to make her own way. Uneducated by worldly standards, she left the shelter of her family and crossed the Channel to stay with her uncle's follower, J.G. Bennett. With help, she opened the first Russian restaurant in London. As it became clearer what she could do best, the restaurant evolved into Luba's Bistro.

With its long tables, eclectic decor, and irrepressible owner-chef, Luba's Bistro was à landmark on the social scene in London for over three decades. Here, a starving artist who might someday paint her portrait devours a plateful of spaghetti next to a member of British royalty enjoying a bit of ordinary life. In the corner, a young truth-seeker follows her every move, gathering up his courage to ask Mr. Gurdjieff's niece a question of tremendous personal import. All were treated alike — welcomed, and fed, and told to finish up, please, because, after all, look at the queue waiting to get in.

There are other stories Luba doesn't tell. They are too private, too self-assuming, but they often show the unexpected outcome of her generosity. Her godson, George Bennett, son of J. G. Bennett, told me two of them. During the early Bistro days, Luba had taken a lonely young boy under her wing, becoming his "second mother." He became a successful, wealthy businessman. Hearing that Luba had developed heart disease after her retirement from the Bistro, he arranged for her care by the best heart specialist in London, delivering her to the most exclusive private hospital in his Rolls-Royce.

She returned to her London flat, and she and her husband, Arthur, resumed the daily care of her elderly landlord with whom they shared the building. They had seen "the old man" through a long series of illnesses and hospitalizations. During one of his hospital stays, his relatives, believing the doctor's prognosis that the end was near, removed everything of value from his home. However, he didn't die. He returned home and, discovering the situation, declared that Luba and Arthur were now his family and willed them the house they shared.

These days, Luba and Arthur live in the Suffolk countryside where, for the first time since she left the Prieuré, Luba has her own garden with plenty of her favorite roses and room for Arthur to grow a few vegetables. It is a gentle time, but her fiery, exuberant spirit echoes in her voice as she relives her memories, reminiscing over the course of many long, hot, summer days — interrupted only by her wonderful meals. Luba makes no claims to hidden knowledge. The best-kept secrets in this book are the recipes which made her Bistro justly famous. But her story speaks to those who wonder what it would be like, as her uncle's teaching suggests, living one's ordinary life in harmony with one's inner life.

Luba's memoirs are full of names, places, and ideas associated with Gurdjieff's teachings. Rather than interrupt her story to explain them, I suggest that readers interested in learning more about this enigmatic man and his work at the Prieuré and in Paris consult the following books. G. I. Gurdjieff wrote several under the title *All and Everything*, best begun by reading the *First Series — Beelzebub's Tales to His Grandson*, and then the *Second Series — Meetings with Remarkable Men*. There are also numerous books by his students and followers, including *In Search of the Miraculous* by P. D. Ouspensky; *Our Life with Mr.Gurdjieff* by Thomas de Hartmann; *Gurdjieff: Making a New World*, and *Idiots in Paris*, which are two of many books by J. G. Bennett; *Boyhood with Gurdjieff* by Fritz Peters, and James Moore's biography, *Gurdjieff: The Anatomy of a Myth*.

What follows are Luba's own inimitable words, spoken in English, accented by the Russian and Armenian of her childhood, with a dash of French thrown in. They are the words of a bountiful and tranquil spirit, spoken with eyes sparkling, laughter never far away.

Marina C. Bear
Berkeley

Luba and Marina in her kitchen —London (1986)

Her Story

This is my grandma on my mother's side with her son back in Armenia

My Uncle's mother in the garden at Prieuré

This is all of us — the patients and the staff at Berck Plage

When we got better we used to take walks on the beach for exercise. I'm standing up on the right.

ALEXANDROPOL TO LONDON

I was born in Alexandropolos, in Armenia — the capital — but we left when I was about four years old. There was a war there, and we heard the Turkish were coming and that they were very barbaric, killing everybody, so we left. My father, my mother, my one sister, grandmother, grandfather — we all left to come to Tiflis. There we found that Georgia was just beginning to be part of the Russian revolution, but I don't remember a lot about that. My mother told me later that she had been born in the same house where Stalin was born. They used to play in the courtyard. But I was very young in Tiflis. All I remember is watching some planes going up and down, dropping paper down on us — you know, telling that the Russians had made the revolution, that kind of thing.

Then I remember that my grandmother, my cousins, my auntie left Russia and the next year we followed them. We headed straight to the Prieuré at Fontainebleau, where my Uncle was then living with some people who were studying with him. Madame Ouspensky came to fetch us at the station and Madame de Hartmann came along. Imagine how the Prieuré was for us, that big house, after Russia and the revolution — all these hardships and bang bangs. Fontainebleau was something like a dream.

My Uncle had seen me when I was a baby, just born, you know, but this was the first time I remember meeting him. And my aunt, his wife, was still alive. There were all these pupils there and the Work was going on, but we couldn't understand anything, then. I was about seven when we arrived. All of our papers got lost, so Madame de Hartmann arranged for papers for us, but everything was wrong in them. They said I was born in Tiflis on April 3, but it was April 29.

We settled into our life. The other children, my sisters, they went to school, but I never went to school. I don't know — that was Mr. Gurdjieff's idea. I had private lessons with him instead. He made me work like a dog.

But I always liked the kitchen. I remember in the Prieuré, when Madame Ouspensky was living there, I used to go in the kitchen and she used to say, "This one will be a good cook one day."

I remember one day I went in and there was a big pot of fish laying there. I was about nine years old. I was poking around in it and the whole pot came over on me. I was smothered in hot water, in fish stock. It was *fantastic*. Immediately my Uncle came running and put some oil on me, and put me by the fire, burning me again. Oh, how I was screaming; how can they do this to me? And I didn't have one single mark, not one, on me afterward. He just put the oil on me and started grilling me by the fireplace. Next morning it was all gone; not even red. Funny, eh? I don't know what they did, but the oil somehow took the burn out.

I remember I was ten years old; I had my duty to do like everyone else: we worked in the garden, we worked in the kitchen, we worked in the laundry one day. We were all speaking Russian and Armenian. We didn't learn French yet. My poor mother, they put her in the kitchen; she was a cook. She cooked all the time, before the war was started. My father was doing lots of naughty things. I tell you about them later. Being the youngest brother, he was very spoiled, and he had a car and everything else — *mais* he worked hard in the garden, helping there.

When she was eighty-two my grandmother died — she was my father and my Uncle's mother. She was an old witch. And the year after, my aunt died — that was Mr. Gurdjieff's wife. I call the grandmother "old witch" because she didn't ever like us. You see, my father left his first wife to marry my mother, so we were considered the bastards. My father had only one daughter from his first marriage, and she died.

So my grandmother died, and life went on in the Prieuré. In the morning, after we got up we all had our chores. Once a week you would look after his room — my Uncle's room. And that was the worst chore you could ever have, because if his bed was not made perfectly, just the way he wanted it, all the Prieuré would shake. I remember one day I was very little. I had just made his bed. He said "What is that?" I said, "What?" "Do you call that a bed? That's not a bed. You do it again." I was a little kid, and it was a big, big bed. And he sat there, with his arms folded, watching, watching. I made every pleat just perfect, and when I was done, he pulls back the covers and says, "I'm going to bed now." You see his big principle is, you do something, you do it well, or you don't do it at all. But you get a chance to try again. You get many chances.

Then after chores, everybody went to work; the children went to school and Luba was staying home. Thank God I learned how to cook. Twelve o'clock was lunch. The children and grown-ups were eating separately. Then at three o'clock he went to sleep. The Big Master went to sleep and nobody was supposed to move anymore because he was in bed. The children were sent away to the forest and the garden — anywhere.

At five o'clock he used to get up and then we had tea, and after tea more lectures. We had lectures every day. They used to read to us what he was writing about, and after lectures we had Movements, always from five o'clock until eight o'clock. I was about twelve years old when Movements started and I did Movements until he died — twenty years or more. Then it was dinner again and after dinner we did what we wanted to do. You know, there was not much to do there. We used to go to the pictures.

There were quite a few young people there, about ten of us: the four of us in the family and my cousin, and Tom and Fritz Peters — we were all brought up together — and Madame de Salzmann's daughter Busic, and then her son Michel was born.

When I was about twelve I began to have this pain in the back. They took me to all kinds of doctors, but they didn't know what it was. Then I went to a country doctor, a young man, and he took an X-ray and found it was tuberculosis of the bone. They put me into plaster for four years. I went to Berck Plage — it was a place specially made for treating that kind of illness, near Calais.

For four years I was there. Nobody was with me — it was just a big hospital, but they used to come every week to see me and bring me everything. It was the most delightful time of my life, during my trouble. My Uncle would come every week; my father came; they brought me fruit and flowers and spoiled everybody. You know, it was wonderful, because I was spoiled there. I was flat down on my back, plaster from head to foot, and when the plaster finally came off, they put an iron corset on me. I could only use one leg to walk; I was dragging the other one. But after about a year I was walking normally.

So they came and fetch me back to the Prieuré and we stayed there another five years, until the war started. I was not doing too much during this time because I was not very well. Just ordinary Prieuré life going on — lectures and the talk and the yelling and shouting and all that kind of things. It never stops.

Mais my father was *fantastic*, because my father was gambler. He would disappear all night gambling. He used to play bridge, or that French game La Balota. And when he wins, he used to stay all morning until the shops open and bring us all presents. When he used to come very early and sneak in the bedroom, we knew he lost everything.

He used to take a car, go to Paris. And because he was very handsome, very tall and skinny, and he used to like pretty girls, too, my mother used to send me with him. "Go and sit with Papa. See what he's doing." I used to say "God, all right." But my father was clever. He would put me in one picture theater, take me out from one and put me in another. I used to see about seven pictures. And then by midnight I used to come have something to eat, and I sat there and watch and watch until four o'clock, five o'clock, until I say, "I think we better go home." We go home. That was funny. It was my Uncle's fault, really, because my father was the youngest. But when they were young, my father helped my Uncle for his traveling — gave him money and boots and everything else. And when they came to Europe, we knew my father would say "Golya, I lost everything." "Here, have some money."

That was all in secret — we never saw it. But next day he always had money in his pocket.

Then the war came and we lost the Prieuré, because my Uncle didn't have any money there — it was all in America and when the war came he was broke. We gave it up. There is nothing left from those times, except for the photographs. We left everything behind. We all thought we would be going back, that this was just during the beginning of the war.

So my Uncle left Fontainebleau and went back to Paris. He had a flat there. We bought a little house for mother in Fontainebleau. We stayed in Fontainebleau and my Uncle was in Paris and the war had started. We were all very broke. Nobody had anything to eat and I started working. I was a waitress. I was a charwoman. I work in a manufactory, you know, making bombs. I stayed there two years. I worked from six o'clock in the morning until six o'clock in the evening. Later I worked from six in the evening to nine in the morning. When I came home my mother was crying because my hands were so sore. I used to curl them up and go to bed. It was terrible.

But the worst part of my life was when I was a cleaning woman. I couldn't find any other work, and some of the people were really nasty. They were taking me for a kitchen towel. It really hurt. I thought, "Oh, I can learn a couple of things. We need the money." I don't think I went two months and I was finished with it. I was fed up. I said to Mama, "I can't do that any more." It's not like me to give up my job, but I got another one.

And then — what happens now? The funny part. When the Germans arrive, I was traveling all the time between Fontainebleau and Paris to see my Uncle and help him. My cousin Valya used to help him with the cooking, the cleaning, and everything else at the flat. My Uncle was still having some pupils. Madame de Salzmann was there all the time.

When the Americans came into the war I was back in Fontainebleau. We were the last ones — everybody had left. They all said, if the Germans come, they will rape you, kill you, and all that kind of thing. Mother said, "I don't have anything to do with the Germans." So she will stay. In the end, everybody left and we went with them. We took what we could, and we walked sixty miles. We piled everything on two bicycles and we walked sixty miles, to some little village. I don't even know where it was. It was like a sea, and we were carried along, going on and on and on. And suddenly the Germans arrive behind us.

All the roads were completely cleared off, and then a big car came with four Germans in it. I don't know why, but they looked at us and one came very politely and he asked my mother, "Madame, what are you doing?" She said, "Everybody left. We're no soldiers, you can see that." And he was smoking a cigarette. And, you know, I hadn't had a cigarette for three weeks, and I was pulling on mother's leg and I was saying, "Mother, ask him for a cigarette." She said, "No, I can't; I can't." But in the end she said, "Would you please give my daughter a cigarette?" And he smiled at me and he gave me four cartons of cigarettes from somewhere in the car. And I took one and all the French fellows were there around me, all the French people, and they say, "Oh, Mademoiselle, don't smoke them — they must be poison." I say, "I don't care if I'm going to die; I'm going to have my cigarette."

And then the German said to my mother, "Madame, why are you walking like this? I have something to do yet, but if you wait here half an hour then I will come back and fetch you." Mama said, "Oh no, no." But I said the rest of us should walk back and we took the bicycles and we came home, and when we came home our house was not touched.

Suddenly I said to my sister, "We must do something for Mama." We remembered there was a house where a Jewish couple had been living, not far away. They were terribly mean, but they had a beautiful kitchen garden. And we went there and started pulling all the vegetables. The Jewish were all gone by then, you see. And then two big Germans came and they look at us and say, "What are you doing?" I say, "We're trying to make a soup for my Mama." So they helped us, and then it turns out one of them was a cook. He said, "Wait a minute — have you got any meat?" I said, "No." He went and got a big piece of beef, and when Mama came, five, six hours after, there was a big pot of soup.

In the war time, when we stayed in Fontainebleau, I was the only one keeping the family going. When I could, I used to go to Paris because we had a friend who had a bakery and he used to keep all these croissants and cakes he couldn't sell anymore — two, three days-old ones. I used to bring them home and Mama used to put them in the oven, you know, make some kind of pudding. She was a good cook.

I remember we had some Jewish friends, and they were terribly frightened, because at this time they were killing all the poor Jews. We put them in our cellar. They stayed there for five months. We fed them all we could. Afterward, they went to America.

The end of the war, the last six months, that was the most difficult because they were fighting all around Paris — the English came one way and the Americans another and the Germans and the French, and we were surrounded, you see. They never put bombs on Paris, no. *Mais* it was fighting. And then the tanks came, one after another and there was nothing to eat. Of course you could buy anything you want in the black market, if you had the money, but you couldn't just buy anything. To get bread I got up at three o'clock in the morning to go queue until eight o'clock when they open. Everybody was fighting, and I was just standing there, waiting. And then you get a piece of brown bread and sometime you open it and there's a mouse tail or something in there. Well, we used to cut off that little piece and eat the rest of it.

One day, during the war, Mama and I went to the market and when we sat down on the tram I saw a purse full up with money there on the seat. Naturally, I put it in my purse, but I didn't say anything to Mama. She was so honest, she would say to the conductor, "You know, somebody lost this." But I say to myself, "No, you're not going to get this one." When we came home, I said, "Mama, look what I found." It had about ten pounds in it — which was quite a lot of money in that time. Mama said, "You must go to the police." I said, "I'm not going to the police." "You can't keep it," she says. We were broke like hell. I said, "People who can walk with all this money in a purse must have money hidden."

Anyway, she put a little advertisement in the newspaper for one week, that if anybody lost that purse, come and get it, but nobody ever came. It must be somebody was black market or something, you see. Anyway for three or four months we were rich. We could buy a little bit of black market food and Mama bought us shoes. I remember later walking in shoes and my toe was coming out.

That's why I started making shoes, because you couldn't buy dresses and shoes. I used to make shoes for all my family. I could buy cork and cover it with material. It used to look very professional. The shoes used to go with your dress. We were very elegant. Later on, we had an old shoemaker, Mr. Schweit. He was very nice. He used to put a little rubber sole on it. I used to make straps with the same color, like Egyptian shoes. I remember my fingers had all holes in them, because you used that big needle. *Mais* I made them. It was fun. It was a challenge. You must have a challenge, otherwise you die if you don't pull yourself out.

We used to go into the forest, my sister and me, five minutes from the house, and get wood three times a week. We cleaned that forest. But there used to be people in the forest sometimes. They said there were very bad people — Algerians — and they could rape us, kill us. So we used to take my dog. He was a lovely Alsatian. One day we were picking up branches and we heard someone coming. It was a very big man. I took hold of the dog and I said, "You come to us and I'm going to put the dog on you." And the dog started roaring and the man turned and ran away.

It was another something funny — you know the Germans took the dogs. They took them to the front to use for sending messages, or something. They took my dog and I didn't see him two years. But in Fontainebleau there was a nice walk from us to the railroad station and then to the Hotel Savoy. That had been a very nice hotel, requisitioned by the Germans. One day I was walking by there and suddenly I hear a dog crying his head off and I say, "It's impossible. It can't be Hooch. It can't be my Hooch."

He was there, and he felt I was coming. And he was so happy — he was barking and barking and barking. There were two soldiers holding him, and I say, "Please, can I see the dog. I think it's mine." They look at me and they think I am completely crackers, so they say, "Yes, you go." He was my dog. I never gave him to them. But what happened to him after I never found out. He was a lovely dog. He used to hate these old women — anybody in black he used to go for them, but he was so gentle with the children.

Finally, I got a job taking care of children. I really liked that — I stayed six months. She was American and he was French. I didn't know it at the time, but he worked for the Germans. It was very difficult, because we needed jobs to live, you know. But there was the liberation — everybody called them the fee-fee, soldiers sixteen, seventeen, fourteen years old — they would take anybody who slept with a German or had anything to do with the Germans. They would shave their heads in front of everyone. I had two friends, an English and a French girl, and they shaved their heads and put glue on them and put feathers, like a chicken.

I was working with the Germans because I didn't have anything else. Everyone said to my mother, "Take your girls and go to Paris, because here they are going to have a bad time." So we left from Fontainebleau and went to Paris. First we stayed with my Uncle, and then he put us in two rooms in a hotel. During the war he had only some French students with him, and Madame de Salzmann. Her husband had died a long time before at the Prieuré.

We lived for months in the hotel. I worked as a waitress in a coffee shop. I liked that. It was nice, selling tea and coffee and cakes. I used to do the coffee job from one o'clock to six o'clock; then from six to midnight I was cashierette at a cinema. I did that in Fontainebleau after the war, too. That was the worst part, because all the people who were in Fontainebleau — the mayor, all the rich people — they used to come to the Prieuré for Christmas, for parties, all these young people, you see. And now they would come to the cinema and I was working there, selling oranges and ice cream, and they would give a little extra money and say, "There, that's for you." How many times I came home with tears in my eyes, but I say, "No. I'm going to stick with it. I don't care. It's honest work."

Then one day I was in the cinema and one of the girls dropped some pennies in my tray and said "That's for you," and I was really angry. She was a big girl. I said to her, "I'm not a whore! I do all honest work in my life!" She went all white and red and yellow and she said to the manager, "She attacked me." He said, "You mean Luba attacked you? She's the nicest woman I ever had in this cinema." (I was kind. I was well brought up, you know.) We went in his office and I told him what had happened. He went back and said to the girl, "You, madam, never come back in this cinema again. I don't want your custom." Oh, it was terrible.

When the war was finished and everything was all right, money came back from America and my Uncle started living like always. But he never got his Prieuré back. It was taken by the Germans, and afterwards the French took it to make a rest home for old people. But he was not angry. He said that was the past; we must do the future, now. No, he was not angry at all. I don't think he wanted to go back there anyway. He was a man for whom if something didn't work, he goes further on. He would start a new life. So after the terrible war, it was time to start a new life. He kept his flat in Paris and started traveling all over again. He always traveled.

We had funny lives. Sometimes we forget we were kids once; we were naughty, too, sometimes. I remember we girls wanted to wear lipstick. I was not allowed to wear lipstick until I was eighteen, but we wanted to wear it. When I was sixteen we used to go out and put it on anyway and my Uncle would say, "What is that rubbish on your face?"

He had a girlfriend, my Uncle. She was French-Russian — a funny woman. She wore more makeup than anyone else I have ever seen in the world. It was like paint. I would say to my Uncle, "Why can she do it and not me?" He would say, "When you're her age you can whore yourself." During the war, that woman was making false eyelashes. I worked with her some, and I learned. Gosh, it was difficult work; it was very minute. We used to use our own hair and fasten it to little wooden mats. She used to work for Elizabeth Arden.

I had long eyelashes — people used to poke fun when I was a kid. But I started wearing these false ones, too. In Paris, I was photographed with these eyelashes on. It was fun, but I couldn't see to read the newspaper with them on, they were so long and thick. I had beautiful eyes when I was young. They were very Oriental, very black. I was very proud of my eyes.

Once you could travel again after the war, Mr. Bennett (that was J. G. Bennett) was coming all the time to France. All the English followers of my Uncle were coming to France, coming in and out. I had always wanted to come to England, but I was terribly frightened to ask my Uncle, because I thought he will kill me. It took me three months just to think how to do it, then one day I just took all my courage and I ask him. Because Mr. Bennett said, "Anytime you come, you are welcome at Coombe Springs."

So one day my Uncle was sitting and smoking, and I say, "I want to talk to you, Uncle." And he said, "What do you want?" I say that I want to go to England. And you know, for the first time in my life he just jumps forward: "You want to go to England!" And I was frightened of him, you see. But it's something I want to do. You see, I never realized, in all these things, if you want to do something yourself, you must just do it. And immediately, two days after that, I had my passport, I had the money, they telephone to Bennett's and I left France. I never went back there to live.

I arrived in England. I stayed with Bennett in Coombe Springs. At that time old Mrs. Bennett was still alive. She was in her seventies. She was twenty three years older than he was. She was *fantastic*. I started working at Coombe, cooking, like always. I'm twenty-eight years old now, and it's my first time out in the world. I was only three months in England when my Uncle died. We chartered a plane and went back to France to bury him. It was all very unexpected. He had some trouble with his legs, with his walking, something like that. They called a doctor from America and he did the wrong thing and Uncle had a heart attack. But he was eighty-two.

When my Uncle died, my mother was there. On his deathbed, my Uncle said to Madame de Salzmann — because he knew she would take care of everything — he told her, "Don't forget the family." He knew what she was planning. We never had anything, except from Uncle. He kept the whole family together. During the war, I helped with money from my jobs, but it was Uncle who kept the family together. He was our bread and butter. He bought us what we needed, more than my father did.

So after Uncle died and was buried, first his flat in Paris was completely closed up. Nobody was allowed to go in. When he died in hospital, my mother was in the hospital with him. Madame de Salzmann was already arranging everything. There was a young French girl who has been looking after him; she was already there in the flat, filling up suitcases. When we arrived, the flat was empty. Only a few knickknacks were left.

We wanted to sell the flat. They asked us if they could keep it for a museum. When I hear them say they're going to do a museum, I think, "With what? There's nothing left. Everything was pinched." My mother, being a good person, said, "If they want to keep it for a museum, keep it that way. I've got respect for Mr. Gurdjieff." So they kept it, and they call it a museum, but you can't get in. The last time I was in Paris, I went around and rang the bell. The concierge said, "Oh, Madame, you can't go upstairs, it's locked." I said, "I thought it was a museum." "Yes, sometimes people come, but only with special permission."

I rang up Madame de Salzmann to say I'd like to go in the flat. She was not there. "Madame is not available," they said. I said, "Listen, my name is Gurdjieff. Luba Gurdjieff. And I want to go to the bloody flat." "Oh. Oh. I don't know. I will ring you up." I gave my hotel number, and I sat there for half a day. Seven years later, I'm still waiting. I thought, when I write my book, I want to tell people about this.

Being stupid, as we were then, we really expected that they would continue to help us — to help the family. There was money then, and there is much more money now. The only one who seemed to care after his death, who did anything to help us a little, was Bennett. After that, for twenty years, we never heard a thing. Nobody — none of them ever thought, "What's happening there? Are they all right?" Then they sent us some money. It used to come once a year. It used to be my little nest egg in America. But they never tell how they decide how much, and then last year it's less than half. Why? All the records they sold — I don't know how many — you know how much we had each? Five hundred pounds. That's why we took à lawyer for the family, but he said he couldn't do anything. All the papers are in America. We would have had to pay the lawyer to go to America and do all the research there. Who had the money to do that? Thousands of pounds. Can you imagine the millions of my Uncle's books they have sold? The royalty we have — a couple of weeks ago, I had a hundred pounds. The bank said it was there. "What is this?" "Royalties for the book." A hundred pounds. I spend that going to the supermarket.

Sometimes when Madame de Salzmann came to London, she would invite me for lunch, but we never talked about anything.

Well, after my Uncle's death, we came back to England and my life started going much the same, working, working. I followed Mr. Bennett's work closely. He had followers living in Coombe, the same as in the Prieuré — working and cooking, and there were lectures, all that kind of thing. Nothing was changed for me, anyway, so I start thinking about my future. I wanted to get out from there. I was feeling inside, that I must leave.

Then I met a young man and we were married. I was thirty-three years old. He was a student of Mr. Bennett's, very intellectual. The marriage lasted only seven years.

When I got married, somebody loaned me some money to open a restaurant and that's how that part of my life got started.

This is my mother — how she looked
when I was a teenager

That's Madame de Salzmann in
the middle at the Prieuré

We always played around the
animals. That's Nicholas on the
donkey and my sister Lida holding the
tail. The little boy on the left is
Michel Salzmann.

My cousin Valya and my sister Genia

By this picture we're really settled
in to life in France. This is my
sisters and my cousin and me.

Here is the Prieuré in the winter
with ice in the fountain

CHÂTEAU DU PRIEURÉ

Many times people ask about what was life like in the Prieuré with my Uncle, so I think I should tell a little more about that. It was his School, you know, and many people came and stayed there for a while, and leave and come back. But for us it was home. It was a big château, on the outskirts of Fontainebleau, near the forest.

When we first came to the Prieuré it was so strange. This big house, big garden, and it was summer, full of flowers, roses and everything else. People were looking at us, you know: "Poor little things, just come from Russia." They were all trying to give us sweets.

We had our own house there, three stories tall. There were not many children at the start; Tom and Fritz Peters came later on. My Uncle had been there less than three years when we arrived. My aunt, his wife, was very ill already. She had cancer; she died of it. I never remember her walking; she was always in bed. I remember a big bedroom with a big bed, and she was always very cheerful and very smiling. I remember running in her bedroom and giving her a big kiss, and she would say, "Oh, my little gypsy," because I was so fat and curly-hair.

We adjusted little by little. We adjusted. You do that — children especially. We start running everywhere — to the goats, the dogs, the cows. My Uncle had a horse and he bought us some donkeys. And we had pigs and chickens. My cousin Valya was in charge of the farm part — the horses and cows. The stables were always very clean. That writer, Katherine Mansfield, who was so ill — she was staying above the stables. It wasn't even a room up there — just a place where they could store hay, but open, no walls to close it up.

Valya had had a terrible time as a child. His family didn't leave Alexandropol when we did before the Turks invaded and when the soldiers came they killed everybody that was there except for my cousin, Valya, who was hiding in the hay with the baby, a three-months-old baby. He saw everything happen — they raped my aunt in front of the children, they cut off her father's head, then they killed all the other children.

When they left, Valya took the baby and started walking. He carried that baby for three days, but he had nothing to feed it and the baby died. Valya was ten years old. He walked, sometimes he hid on a train. He was starving; he was beaten.

Anyway, I was playing in the courtyard in Tiflis and suddenly there was this boy, skinny like anything, dirty, covered with vermin. He said, "I am Valya; where is Mama?" I suddenly got very frightened. I start going down the staircase, shouting, "Mama, Mama, there's a beggar outside. He wants to see you." They brought him in and they didn't know who he was. They washed him and everything else and Mama put him to bed. She said, "He looks like Valya." The minute he opened his eyes, he said, "Auntie, it's Valya," and he fainted again.

Two or three days after, he woke up. We didn't have much to eat, because the revolution was on, but we offered him what we had and he was wolfing it down, because he was so hungry. Mama was so startled. Finally a few days later he was able to tell us the horrible story of what happened. Imagine — ten years old, what he saw. And then somehow he had come two thousand miles to get to us. He lived with us after that and came with us to France.

At first, when my grandmother was alive, we all used to go in the living room after we finished dinner. The big fireplace was made up, especially in the winter, and we all sat around my grandmother and the grown-ups used to talk, to tell us stories, and we would sing songs. Then Uncle would say, "It's time for bed," and we used to run to bed. It was a real family life. Most nights there would also be some music. Mama used to play the piano, de Hartmann used to play piano and violin.

They would always start with my Uncle's music. It was very boring for us. Very boring. And then when they finished with this, we could do anything we want. Sometimes we had dancing — we were never forbidden to have a good time.

Later, when more people came, it was a little different. But dinner was for eating and enjoying it. I don't ever remember talking about the Work then. It was: "How do you like that? You want some more? You eat some more." That kind of thing. Sometimes after they finished dinner and they had coffee or something to drink, then they start talking. We were not there. We went out.

The only thing we got, it was the *lecture*, the reading. Somebody was reading something by my Uncle. Not my Uncle — he was never reading — but somebody else was reading fragments of his books, as he wrote them. It's *ridicule*. I was fed up with it. When you are a kid, eight, nine, ten, when you have no education and people come and read you *All and Everything, Beelzebub*, you can't understand anything. First thing, you are sitting on the floor. I used to go to sleep. I don't know how it went in, *mais* it went.

Oh, well, later in my years I was more interested. I started seeing what's happening around me. My father was not interested at all in what was going on there. He used to say, "You're talking rubbish." My Uncle used to love my father, but they used to fight like dog and cat about everything. My father would never agree with my Uncle and my Uncle would never agree with him. You see, my father was a bon viveur. He used to go out all the time, play cards, drink — enjoy life. They looked very much like each other, *mais* you'd never think it was two brothers. They didn't have at all the same ideas.

My Uncle helped a lot of people with money — poor Russian people who didn't have anybody else. But at the Prieuré, when people with money used to come, he would tell them, "I don't want a check with two or three zeros. I want a check with four zeros." And people would do it. In the Prieuré, he always seems to have quite a lot of money. Madame de Hartmann was in charge of it — paying the bills and all that. During the war he had very little, of course. And we left so many things behind in the Prieuré — all those Oriental carpets. You know the Study House was top to bottom with them. There were hundreds, from Persia and India, and we left without taking one. We never thought about it. My Uncle said we would come back one day and who cared about carpets when the war was coming?

When I think about it, when people ask me about it, I know there must have been many well-known people who came to the Prieuré, but we were just there. It was our home, you know?

I remember one American woman, a nice, big lady. She came to the Prieuré in a big Rolls-Royce with a chauffeur and a footman. I'll never forget her silk dress, with a train, how they used to have them. Mr. Gurdjieff came out to see her. She said she wanted to stay with him. He said, "All right, but first you send the chauffeur away and the footman and the car must go — we don't want it here." She said, "You mean my Rolls-Royce?" He said, "You can put it in the garage; you can't use it here."

That woman had never done anything. One day she asked me where do cabbages grow — on trees or under the soil? And do you know her first job was in the morning when she got up. She had on a beautiful dress and all the makeup and everything. My Uncle looked at her. "Are you going to the ball?" he asked. She said, "No, I've come to Work." He said, "Go and put on an old dress." She said, "I haven't got an ordinary dress." He called my Mother and said, "Anna, have you got any rubbish to give her to put on?"

We dressed that woman in an old dress and an apron and a thing on her head. She looked like another woman; you wouldn't have recognized her. "Now," my Uncle said, "you are going to clean all the lavatories." She did it. She stayed and she loved it. She really came to us because she had everything in the world money can buy. She had had about four husbands. Later she was giving it all away. She would give diamond rings: "You want it, you can have it. I don't want it anymore."

One day my mother said, "No, you're not going to give these things away. Anything you want to give away, you give it to me. I'll put it away for you. The day you go away from here, you can have it all back." My mother said it wasn't fair for her to give it all away just because she was finding something here. So my mother took all her jewelry and packed up her dresses. That woman stayed with us five, maybe six years. She didn't want to go, but one day my Uncle said, "You've had enough. Now you must go." And just like that, she left. But she would always write me, and she would come back every year for a few days. She told my mother, "You know, Anna, he's fantastic. I feel like I'm another person."

Lots of people visited — people now I know they are famous. That writer, Bertrand Russell, he visited.

We had a man who came from America. He was paralyzed — he couldn't walk. My Uncle looked after him. He started standing a little bit — walking a little bit. Later I learned it was Franklin Roosevelt. I still wonder whether it was true or not. Because I saw Roosevelt when he went back to America and it was the same man. I don't think anybody else knows that. It was all done so hush-hush. When he left, and he became

President of the United States, and I said "Gosh! It's Teddy!" Funny, ha? I used to call him Teddy — I don't know why; because he was a big boy with a very beautiful face. It was about 1923 when he came to the Prieuré. I tell you, I know it's Roosevelt, but nobody talks about it. To this day I don't know for sure whether it's true or not.

You see, some people came there anonymously, because they didn't want to have known what my Uncle did with them, when they left.

But for us it was just life, going on. My Uncle used to have his own dining room, a huge one, with a table could hold maybe thirty, thirty-five people, and his own chair, there. All the big people used to be invited. He would say, "You come and have lunch with me." Every day it was the same thing, with different people — people coming and going. That dining room was specially for meeting with my Uncle. Then all of the workmen were eating separately and the children were also separate, depending on how big or small they were.

It was the same kitchen, but behind it was a big place, like a study, and we used to eat there. Everybody would eat the same thing. But sometimes Uncle would have caviar and very posh things. He used to have the caviar coming from Istanbul — real Turkish caviar, and Russian caviar. Kilos. It was in the fridge. He used to take a piece of bread and a mound of caviar on it. I was fed up with caviar.

But the food was very ordinary food in my Uncle's place. He used to do lots of Russian cutlets, you know, with chopped meat. He used to do lots of stews. When he could find it, he used to do head cheese. He used to do salads, boiled potatoes. We never had many vegetables. We used to have lots of *zakuskies* for starters. He would use salty herring and lots of onions. Russian salads. I used to make lots of sardines. We'd grill a piece of bread, put sardines on it, and grill it again. That was really good.

We never had steaks or anything like that. It was real peasant food. I remember my mother sitting and making *galubtzy* for a whole day for everybody at the Prieuré. We used to eat lots of rice — everything was done with rice. *Galubtzy*, you must have rice; *supreme*, you must have rice; *blanquette*, you must have rice. He used to like his roast pork — a whole piglet you put in the oven. He used to cut it up and give everybody a piece. That was with rice, too. Not a big pig — a baby pig.

The dinner table was always so nice. Silver and beautiful plates and always beautifully clean cloths. The dining room where he eats was always beautifully laid out. You know who does the washing of all these cloths, yeah? And the floors — we used to have parquet floors. Once a week five of us had to take a big iron thing and polish it all. Oh, God, so much polishing! Madame Ouspensky used to come and say, "Oh, it's not quite good enough, yet." And my Uncle used to say, "That's not good enough; that's not good enough." So many people nearly broke their necks on those floors. One day my Uncle fell on his bottom. Nobody laughed, but we were so amused. He never said anything.

But there was so much fun, too. When we came to him for pocket money, he never just gave. He would stand on that big lawn and throw money up in the air and all the children would rush at it and pick up, pick up, pick up. He enjoyed watching that.

One year we were invaded by slugs that would eat all our vegetable garden. There were ten kids there by then. Uncle gave every one of us a bucket and said, "Now you're all going to collect slugs and the one who collects the most will get a big prize." So off we went. We didn't sleep at all that night, because the slugs came at night. It was raining, but I remember I collected five buckets of slugs. But we all cheated. We were supposed to collect them only in the kitchen garden, but we went into the forest.

Next day, Uncle said, "Now you must count them." We all sat down to count. We were stealing slugs from each other. "No, that one is mine!" My cousin said he was missing seven slugs, because he had counted his the night before. We said, maybe they ran away. "No, they couldn't," he said, "because I put salt on them."

For two days and nights we collect slugs. It was so disgusting. It was horrible. We sat there counting them, one, two, three. Maybe it was fun for kids. I don't even remember now who won or what the big prize was. But I remember Uncle standing there, watching us count slugs.

At Easter he used to hide the eggs in all the bushes, under the rose bushes. The one who found the most eggs got a prize. That was fun. First there was coloring of the eggs. The children would do it and the best eggs got prizes. That's the way it was with my Uncle. Sometimes I used to cheat and pinch somebody else's egg. There were big prizes — maybe a bicycle or a day's outing. The one with the best egg would get to go on a trip with Uncle, to Nice or somewhere else. Sometimes he would give money.

Easter was the most special holiday. There was always lovely weather and we would go out and have tea parties. We always had *pascha* and *kulich*, and roast pork.

They used to send us out when they killed the animals. They were our pets, those pigs. You know how a pig yells when you kill it — like ten thousand babies screaming together. So they would send us to the pictures, and my cousin would butcher them.

The Prieuré used to have a fountain at the edge of the lawn. Once when there was a big party, they filled the fountain with champagne. All the kids — there were lots of them then — were wearing different national costumes, Georgian, Russian, Egyptian, and we served the people the champagne.

At Christmas, my Uncle always made a big party. They would close the doors and the children would wait in the garden. The girls all had new white dresses. At midnight they opened the big door and there was the Christmas tree with candles and presents underneath for everybody. We would invite all the other children — the chauffeur's daughter, everybody. That's one thing I liked about my Uncle: he used to mix everybody together. That's why in the Bistro I would mix everybody together. It was *fantastic*.

He would give us a little carpet, an Oriental carpet, and a hamper, and we used to bring all our carpets in the big living room. We would open the hamper and prepare a little table. You could choose your own guests. We were all after Mr. Gurdjieff to be our guest, you can imagine. He would have a contest — who could hold their arms outstretched the longest could have him as their guest. I got him once. The other grown-ups were other children's guests. The thing is, we had a good children's time and a good grown-up's time — you know what I mean. Then after the little party we would go and get our presents; there were wonderful presents, around the tree. There were bicycles, everything.

Every fortnight he used to take all the children off on a picnic in the Fontainebleau forest. We all had bicycles then. He would drive in the car with all the picnic and in another car would be the other people, and all the rest of us were on our bicycles. I'll never forget this, because my sister was about three years old. She had a tiny little bicycle. She was in the front, because she was the youngest, and the rest of us would follow. We used to yell at her, "Hurry up!" And we would all go into the forest and have a big picnic. There was always music. It was so *fantastic*, because he was very hard and sometimes he was so gentle. I used to hate him sometime. I used to love him a lot.

One year, he bought a big electric car for the children. It was quite a big car — a grown-up could sit in it, too. But he bought it for us. At least that's what he told us. But you know, he never left that blooming car. He was in it all the time. It was his toy. We got so angry. It was finally falling apart, he drove it so much. We wondered how we could hide the batteries, but we never did.

We did things the way he said we should do them, most of the time. Some rules were very strict, but we were always curious. The Turkish bath always was used on Saturday: from four to eight was for women, from nine to twelve o'clock was for the men. Then after the Turkish bath, the men used to go into the Study House. Everything was prepared for them there — dinner and everything. They would close the door and stay all night, sitting there, telling dirty stories, get drunk, all that kind of thing. No females allowed.

I remember once somebody and I decided we're going to see what they do in there, and we hide ourselves so we can peek out. Then we couldn't get out, because they closed the door. We didn't know what to do; we were stuck there. Then about two o'clock in the morning, I heard my mother calling, "Luba, where are you?" My father went out of the Study House to talk to my mother; "I didn't see her, either." They started really worrying.

While they were talking we sneaked out and jumped into bed, all dressed up. Mama came back into the house and in our room and says, "You! You were not here ten minutes ago!" And she pulls back the cover, and there I am, all dressed up. I told her what we did. "Oh," she said, "they will cut you into little pieces!" It was a man's world, I knew that, but I was just curious about what they did there.

When we got older, we used to go into the forest a lot. We built ourselves a hut in the forest. We pinched some of the best Oriental carpets and made ourselves a nice little hut. For what? For smoking. I used to wait until three o'clock in the morning when my daddy was asleep to pinch a couple of cigarettes.

My Uncle had a horse named Fifi that he used to ride all around the Prieuré to see what everybody was doing. One day we were in that hut, Fritz and Tom and Valya, maybe seven of us, and we hear tooka-tooka-tooka — a horse coming. We knew it was my Uncle. We were scared. We had a little chimney and we tried to cover up and stay without breathing and maybe he wouldn't notice us. You could suffocate in there. Finally the horse passes by and my Uncle didn't see us.

We used to have lavatories as big as sitting rooms in the Prieuré. Sometimes we would go into there and open the window to smoke. Miss Potter was in charge of the children and one day she saw smoke going out of the little window, like something was on fire. She came in and she was terrible. She had hands like shovels. We were so frightened of her. She was supposed to prevent mischief. She would look at us — we were very frightened — and she would say, "I am going to tell Mr. Gurdjieff." And we were waiting every day for what she was going to tell Mr. Gurdjieff; waiting for the Bang, Bang. But she never did. She never punished, really. She would just not give us dessert. So we went back to smoking like hell.

When I was seventeen they made a beautiful party, with an orchestra, lovely music, and my father came and handed me a glass of champagne and said, "Luba, now you can smoke." But, you know, I never smoked when my father was there. I had respect for him.

My father died in Mr. Gurdjieff's flat in Paris. After he died, my Uncle said to us, "Now my children, you have one hour to cry, then it's finished. I don't want anybody to cry after that. I don't want any black. He's gone; he's happy; everybody else be happy." And that was it. He said you must not mourn the dead for more than an hour like that. When it's your time to go, you must go, and that is it.

My father and my sister Lida

Such a nice picture. I'm twelve years old. Not the kind of person who would steal slugs, eh?

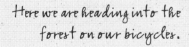Here we are heading into the forest on our bicycles.

UNCLE GEORGE

When I was in the Bistro, people used to come because they heard that I was niece of Mr. Gurdjieff. They look at me like I had three heads. Lots of people thought I was completely cracked. They thought I should sit down and do a big lecture about my Uncle and the Work. They would say, "Talk. Talk to me about your Uncle." I would say, "Listen, here I can't talk about my Uncle. Here I can talk about food. You come here to eat. If you want to talk about my Uncle, you come home when I'm ready." It is so stupid. Can you imagine? I am trying to run my business and they want me to stop and talk about my Uncle.

Kids come and ask me, "What did he really look like?" I don't know. I say, "He was a man." For me, he was a man who so much loves life. He loves everything in life, everything about life. He loves females. He loves children. He loves dogs and cats. And now they are making him a saint. He was not a saint. He was a very, very good philosopher. He traveled all over, learning. He studied in Tibet, everywhere. He knew. But making him a saint? He is not. But people are always looking for some kind of wisdom — some kind of fire coming out. And I was always so dirty; I was always busy working like a stevedore.

When I first went to England, to Coombe Springs, my Uncle used to call there and ask Mr. Bennett how I was doing. Mr. Bennett told him, "Everybody likes her. All the boys are running after her!" He used to say, "Bravo, Luba, that's good. That's good." He began to be nice before he died.

The people who were there with Mr. Bennett, they received me like a queen. They started following me around, asking questions. "Oh, tell us all about Mr. Gurdjieff." I said, "This is such a stupid question. What can I tell 'all about' Mr. Gurdjieff?" It would take me two years to tell all about him. I don't know what to tell, so I say, "He was my Uncle. I liked him very much." "But what kind of man was he?" I said, "He was a dirty old man."

One old man there, he went red like a beetroot. He said I was the most impolite woman in the world.

All the boys were looking after me: "Luba, you come to my party. Luba, I take you out for dinner tonight. Would you like something?" It was Luba, Luba, Luba. And then when my Uncle died, they forgot about Luba. I used to think it was because I was Luba Gurdjieff; now I'm just Luba. I mean, I didn't care about that. All what I did there I did for Mr. Bennett. After all, I was living there for nothing. The other people — well, we used to have a little list in the morning, "Who's Doing What" and when they saw "Luba in the kitchen" they used to say, "Hooray!"

But my Uncle never used to tell us about his life. There was never, "Uncle, tell me the story of the time you did this or that." We didn't have that kind of thing. That's why my life seemed so normal. I never thought about it. It was so natural.

My grandmother used to tell about when my Uncle was a young man. At that time my father was richer than my Uncle. My father had a cinema in Alexandropol, and then he had a shoe shop. He was quite well off. He became mayor of Alexandropol. My Uncle used to come back after all these trips without a penny. Once he came from Tibet — he didn't even have a pair of boots, and so he pinched my father's best boots. Even in France, they were talking about those boots. My father used to tease him. "I had a whole shop full of boots, and you pinch my boots."

My father used to help my Uncle in his traveling, you see. My father worked; he was a family man. My Uncle was all the time going somewhere. He used to come home for one or two weeks and get clothing and money and then he would go. Sometimes it was a couple of years — nobody heard anything, nobody knew if he was alive or dead, and suddenly he would appear again.

When we were children, after we came to the Prieuré, he used to take us to the Riviera, to Cannes, to the best hotels. But we never had anything to wear. It was a funny life. My mother had to ask him over and over to get shoes for us. Because my father was not working, only in the garden. Anyway, my Uncle took us places. We went skiing in Switzerland. I never forget my skiing. I was sitting on my skis and I couldn't move, I was so frightened. My Uncle was sitting on the balcony, watching, laughing his head off. He said to me, "You've always been fat; you'll always stay fat." He used to call me a fat burro.

When we all ate together he used to say to somebody, "Eat, or I put it in the dustbin." He used to call me a dustbin, because I used to eat all the rest. I used to be very angry. Always when we were sitting around, and there would be nice young people, he says, "Come on dustbin, I got something for you." That was me, the dustbin. One day I say, "Now I'm a big girl, I don't want to be call a dustbin." "All right," he said. "I won't call you dustbin." He didn't call me dustbin after that. He knew I'm grown up. Enough is enough.

In spring, we used to go to the south of France. We always had three, four cars going, with maybe twenty people all together. My Uncle would always drive the car in front. He was a rotten driver. My father was a good driver, but my Uncle was rotten. I don't know how he didn't kill himself. He was a terrible, terrible driver (even after his big accident — that happened a year before we arrived in the Prieuré). I would say, "Thank God I'm not in his car." He would drive very slow; then he would go very fast. Then he would pull over by the side of the road and we would have a nice picnic — not just sandwiches, but roast chickens, cucumbers, vegetables.

Mama and I used to prepare it all in advance, packing the baskets — wine for the grown-ups and lemonade for the kids, lots of fruit. We always had *seleyotka* — you know, the salty herrings. Uncle used to like that. We used to have little cakes. We each had our own napkins. It was all quite fun. We would always take the wind-up gramophone with us so we would have music when we ate. Everybody used to swim when we got to the seaside. We took all the dogs with us. It was really an outing.

We used to go always to the same hotels. All the staff used to come out to greet him. "Mr. Gurdjieff is coming." He used to say, "When you give good tips, you are Somebody. If I never gave anything, they wouldn't care about me. It's true." They knew he was somebody special, but I don't think they knew what he was doing. They knew he was shouting and everything was served. They knew he had money. He was coming with his big coat, his big moustache. If he look at you, you could just drop dead — the power in his eyes. That man, I never seen a power like his.

But he did funny things. One day, some place in Monte Carlo, he was eating in a restaurant and they served some kind of chips. My Uncle said, "Who done these chips?" When he used to come, all the staff used to find excuse to go to do something for him because he was money, you know. Three chefs came from the kitchen to tell who done the chips. And then came a little boy, kitchen boy, and he said, "I peeled the potatoes." All the chefs was standing there like that, thinking, "God." And my Uncle took what would be twenty pounds now, and he gave it to the little boy. He said, "You have that money. You deserve, peeling these chips. They were *fantastic*." And the rest were standing there — you can see the faces on those chefs!

He used to make it very difficult for us, sometimes. I remember once I was sixteen years old and we were staying in one of the poshest hotels, the Carleton. I had a very pretty dress, my first evening dress, with flowers. There I was, all nice-nice, with makeup and all that, and my Uncle says that night he's too tired. He's not coming down to dinner. I thought, "Oh, thank God. We're going to have a nice, peaceful dinner." And in the middle of the dinner he comes down with a big tray of watermelon. And he is in his pajamas and dressing gown. He says, "Ay, children, I forgot to give you that for dessert."

If you could see us! We were so annoyed. Everybody in all this jewelry and everything, in front of all these posh people, we were very proud, sitting there, and he goes and messes up everything, coming in his pajamas and slippers.

Next morning I say, "Uncle, how could you do it?" He says, "What did I do?" I say, "You came in your pajamas, and we were sitting in the dining room." He says, "Well, you put pajama in night time. You can put it in daytime — doesn't matter. It was pajamas. Wouldn't change a thing. You must have a little carboozi." (Carboozi was watermelon.)

But he loved children. He used to start all kind of games. He enjoyed that. He used to hide all kind of things in the trees and we were supposed to find them. You know, toys, money, pocket money. He used to bring out the gramophone and we would start dancing.

It was a good life, and it was a bad life — for me, that is. You see, I didn't get what I wanted. I wanted to be a pianist. I used to love piano, and I used to play beautifully. And he didn't want it. Anything I wanted, he didn't want. It was something between him and me. I don't know what it was. I'm very grateful, because he taught me what I know. What I mean is, working with my hands. Nothing with the brain — all with my hands. The brain I got by myself.

You knew whenever he was disapproving. At the Prieuré, I had a boyfriend. He was Georgian. My Uncle knew very well I had a boyfriend and he was very angry, because my boyfriend was not good enough. He never talk about it, *mais* once he said, "My niece could do better than that." And you know, when you're young, don't look like that. You do all kind of mistakes. *Mais* I got married in England, and my Uncle was already dead. I married very late.

Before, I was engaged to a Jewish boy. He was so nice; we were really in love. *Mais* unfortunately the Germans took him in a concentration camp and he died. His mother went with him. That was a very big heartbreak for me.

During the war I didn't have any boyfriends. I had friends I went dancing with, but I didn't care about boyfriends. Funny — you know, I think it was my mother's bringing me up. Because my mother was so pure. When my father died, she was only thirty-nine. She was beautiful and so many men ask her to marry. She say, "No, I never marry. My life is for my children." She never got married. We used to say, "Please, Mama, marry a rich man." But she never did.

But my Uncle never changed. Not in my eyes, anyway. He was still a big bully.

People used to come to my Uncle, and he would say to them, "Why do you come? If you've got a reason why you come, then you can stay. If you haven't got a reason, please go." You know what my Uncle used to say? "If you're poor, you don't pay anything. The rich will take care of things." And that was quite sensible, don't you think? Some poor bugger comes; he can't pay. Are you going to put him out? No. That was the policy of my Uncle and I think it was so just. If you are poor, and it is there, give it to them. It doesn't cost you; let the rich people pay for it.

Of course, during the war we were all very poor. The people in America were very concerned because they didn't know what was happening to us. People thought my Uncle was arrested, because he was with the French resistance. He was not at all with the Germans, you see. He had so many high connections; he was quite well-known in Paris. That's why he was never arrested. They came two or three times for him, but they never arrested him, thank God.

We were all very poor, *mais* we ate well. You know why? Because all the people who supplied him with food, they still supplied him for four years. They knew that one day he will pay them back. He owed so much money; I don't know how much he owed when the war ended. Then the Americans came back and he paid all his debts.

But there were always stories and rumors about him. People said he was a spy, was a Rasputin. When we were in the Prieuré, we used to have sheep heads. You know, that's very Oriental. All the poor people had sheep heads. You wash them nicely, then you put it in the oven, then you grill it. It's beautiful. The brains and everything. People used to say that my Uncle ate children's heads, that he was killing the children. It was so mysterious, what was happening in that place, that château. When I was a kid, some people even called me a baby-eater. I would say, "Mmmmmm, they're so good." I was a devil. When I was riding on my bicycle up the big hill to get to the Prieuré, as I would ride by people would say, "Oh, it's the children-eater!"

But with my Uncle, things always went his way. We just did it. Like the coffee — you know, that story about him writing and the coffee is always getting cold. It was just like that. It was regular coffee, not Turkish coffee. How many times I had to change that coffee! If I did it now, I would have put it in a thermos.

Of course in Paris he was going nine o'clock to the Café de la Paix and sitting there and observing everybody and writing his book. I know, because many, many times I was having coffee with him, and then I go away, go shopping, and come back and he is still there. Until one o'clock he used to sit there, writing, always on sheets of paper. He never had a notebook or anything proper. Other people kept track of it. He didn't even know how to write properly; he never had a formal education. But he took everything he could that people had to offer him. He knew what he was talking about. Many times there were other people around, Mrs. de Salzmann, de Hartmann, Ouspensky, Orage was there. Later there would be readings from what he wrote — sometimes in French, sometimes in Russian, but more often in French, because there were more French people there. When we had some Americans it was occasionally in English. They were translating all the time after he wrote.

The English, they didn't know how to say his name. They called him Mr. GOOR-jeef, Mr. Gurr-DJEV, Mr. GURR-jeff, Mr. Gurr-JEV. Finally the English people staying there started to call him Gyorgi Ivan'ch, like the Russians who knew him. Nobody ever called him by his first name — only my family, my father. When I wanted something from him, I would always say "Uncle." The "Mr. G." business is just what Ouspensky put in his book. He made it up. Although a long time later, Madame de Salzmann started using that —

"Mr. G." But I never heard that in the Prieuré. I think maybe the first time I heard that was at Coombe Springs. I think some people couldn't really pronounce GYOOR-JEFF very well. Idiots.

Oh, we had twenty-one idiots! My Uncle used to make a toast to every kind of idiot. It was a square idiot, a round idiot, a long idiot — oh, I don't know all of them. Somebody must remember all this idiot. He used to tell people what kind of idiot they were. I was a round one, because I was idiot all the time. I didn't drink all those toasts, but he used to say, "She's a round idiot." My cousin, all the family was round idiots. My father, though, he was good/bad/good/bad idiot.

After all these idiot toasts we had so many armagnac bottles at the Prieuré! One day he get the idea to cut all the bottles, take the top off and the bottom and plant flower buds in them. When you used to come there was a nice little garden with a big fountain and then he stuck all these things round with the flowers. Hundreds of bottles of armagnac, empty. Imagine all the boys sitting there, trying to cut those things. So many people cut themselves and bleed like hell. So we had a bottle garden. Pretty soon you couldn't see what it was, because the flowers grew all over. One thing — my Uncle loved flowers. He was always looking after his garden, telling where to plant the special roses.

People ask me: "Did he change? All the years you were with him, did you notice him changing?" It's very difficult when you live with someone. I mean people come. They say, "Luba, you haven't changed." But they don't see my body, how it's changing, getting weaker. But he never changed. It was always the same bloody thing. Never change. Even when he was getting older. Shouting and yelling and eating well and drink well. Still driving a car. After all, he died when he was eighty-two. He still was driving a car.

I'm very thankful for what he taught me, because I would never be alive if not for him. I'm very sorry my Uncle died before I opened the Bistro. He would be proud of me. But I tell you something — he was always there. My father not so much, I'm sorry to say. My mother and my Uncle are always with me.

About five years ago I was very sick in my chest. I was coughing; I couldn't breathe. My husband, Arthur, was sitting with me. I said, "Go to bed, darling." I was really sick. I couldn't lie down, only sit. And suddenly I woke up and I saw my Uncle there. Standing there, with his hat on — his Astrakhan hat. He said, "Don't worry, girl, you'll be all right." I said that I couldn't breathe. He said, "Don't worry, darling, you'll be all right. Now get some sleep." I went to sleep, and the next morning I felt ten times better. I said to Arthur, "I'm hungry." I hadn't eaten anything for a couple of days. I said, "I think I dreamed about my Uncle last night." But it wasn't a dream. He was there. He was there with his hat, standing by me. I just opened my eyes and he was there. After that, I got better and better and then I was all right.

I know some people used to think he had some kind of magic powers. That makes me really angry. He was not a magician. I know he was a healer. I saw him do it, with his eyes. I remember a woman came one day. She was very ill, very weak. He just looked at her, just to calm her, I think. He had very powerful eyes — frightening. People sometimes tell me I have my Uncle's eyes. I say, "No. No, I don't want them." The eyes — you can even see it in the photographs of him.

Sometimes it is so false — the things people write about him, so horrible. I read the books Fritz Peters wrote. He's dead now, the poor man. When he was describing the Prieuré, it was he who was doing everything. He was looking after Mr. Gurdjieff; he was doing the cooking; he cleaned the bathrooms; he was doing the gardening. And I look at him: he never did anything much, the silly bugger. But what he is writing is nothing like what it was. He rang me up from America once. "Did you read my book?" I said, "Yes, it gave me lots of laughs." You know what he did? He hung up on me.

But the main thing I want to do — I want to tell about the man he was. I want to tell that my Uncle was not a saint. I want to tell that he was a man. He was not just clever — he was a philosopher. But why do they want to make him a saint? He loved life. He used to have sex everywhere he went. He has children all over the world. He likes drinking. He was alive. He was more alive than anyone I've ever seen. I loved him. I like him. I admire him. He was *fantastic.*

In the middle of a trip, my Uncle would have us just stop by the side of the road. I never knew why.

But sometimes we'd have a picnic in a field during his trips. That's not me on the right, it's my cousin Pushka.

I can't remember who the fellow was, but I loved riding on his motorcycle!

My Uncle in his Astrakan hat

My Uncle in Paris

WORKING IN LIFE

One day in the Bistro somebody says to me, "And what about the Work?" I said, "Here is the Work." They never understood what is Work. If you do something, and you do it well, and you like it, it is the biggest satisfaction you can have. You give something in life. That is my Work.

When I was growing up, for me it was all natural. People can't seem to understand. For me, it was the natural world. It was the only world I knew. I didn't have to make any pilgrimage. It was life. It was fantastic; it was bad, it was good. Sometimes I thought he made too much work for us, but I always knew that other people thought this was something special. They were coming on these pilgrimages. When I was about fourteen, I started understanding more.

You see, I was brought up in the Work — what they call the Work. But I am not spiritual. I don't like using all this spiritual talk. I know my Uncle helped me lots with spiritual things, because he was always there, fathering. Work was so much a part of my life, I thought it was natural. I didn't understand why everybody didn't do it, too. I was surprised when I learned people didn't do it. It was something that was there. It was natural. If you have an apple, you eat it. It is just what you do.

When I see other people doing anything, I want to know, why don't you do it well? What are you doing? If you are drinking something, this glass of water, then you enjoy the glass of water while it's here. You know, the little things are more important, often, than the big things — for me. You live by the little things. Life gives you something good, something bad — take it as life gives it to you and then make it more so.

You know, they were really eating very bad at Coombe Springs when I got there. Then they started getting better, because I did not ruin the food, you know. There was a woman there, she used to hate me. When I arrived, I said, "Can't you do better?" Everything she needed was there. I said, "Can't you do better than this?" After all, it was about 150 people every day. It wasn't even English cooking; I don't know what it was. She would make a stew, it was all runny, not tasty at all. Never any herbs, even though there were so many herbs in the garden.

So I said to Mr. B. "Can I cook?" He said, "Do you want to?" I said, "Yes, I want to." He said, "You can do it, but not every day." I said, "No, I won't do it every day, but I will cook." And when they tried my cooking, Mr. B. said, "You can have all the people you want." He knew it took a staff to do things like *galubtzy*.

I think that was how I was able to start my Bistro. I learned about organization in the kitchen in the Prieuré and then more at Coombe. I used to say, "You do the cabbage that way, and you do this and you do that." I used to show them how to do it. And then I'd put it in a pot and then I'd make my sauces. I always said to them, "You must fiddle your cooking." You know what I mean by fiddle — being creative.

Mr. B. really appreciated the improvements in the food. I remember one day I didn't cook; somebody else cooked spaghetti. I was out. He never would yell at me, because he was trying to be a little Gurdjieff, you know. I came into the study, and everyone was sitting down, and I sat down and he yelled at me, "Luba, what is this rubbish?" I looked at him, "What are you talking about?" Everybody was shaking. Everybody was always shaking; I didn't understand why. "This is really rubbish on this table." I said, "Well, if you want to eat it, you eat it. I didn't do it. And you don't yell at me like that!"

I didn't act special because I was Mr. Gurdjieff's niece, because I was a nice kid. I did everything he wants. But I told Mr. B., when I come to England, nobody yells at me. Because I was fed up to here with that. "Oh no, nobody will." But he was so unhappy that time. I didn't do it! Marjorie did it! He was going to have to throw out all that food. He didn't say he was sorry then, but afterwards he came and took me in his arms, and, "Darling, darling, sorry. . . ."

You see, even in that kind of a system there was jealousy. She was jealous because people loved my cooking. I used to say, "Little Margie, I know how to cook. I've been in the kitchen since I was born. I like it. I do something, I do it." Later that day, I was out, I don't know where, and she cooked something of mine. I said, "Oh, bravo, Margie." But then I taste it, and it was not at all the same thing. It was dry.

I don't say I'm a wonderful cook. I just like cooking and what I do, I do it well. I'm trying, anyway. I'm sloppy, but it's good. It is who I am, who I was. It is me. It is not how I was brought up. There were three sisters, and no one is the same. I always thought I didn't belong in my family. My attitudes were different. I worked harder, I was a perfectionist. Mama always used to say she found me in the bushes somewhere, in the rose bushes. They called me the gypsy.

Who wants to be like an angel? You must be good and bad sometimes, because life gets monotonous. Not Bad-Bad, *mais* wicked. How you say in English "wee-ked." I was very wicked. I remember, even my mother used to say, "I don't know how you get out of it." "I don't know," I say, "I just get out."

Some people can be a little wicked, but no one takes notice; they know it doesn't come from the heart. Other people are wicked from the heart, and that's horrible.

My sisters say, after all, I didn't have much life. For them, my life was always a silly life. Silly. I'm a silly woman. I laugh too much. I love too much. I have too many friends who love me. They're silly because they love me. After all, what have I got? I know how to do a few things. I try to do them well.

But that's why, later on, in the Bistro, if anybody complained in that place, I was so sure that everything was fresh and good. You can complain because you don't like it, not because it isn't good. That's another question. They could never say the steak was rotten or the salad wasn't crispy. Everything was perfect. I like everything perfect. I like to do things perfect. Sometime I would start doing things halfway — I was tired; I'm not young anymore — but I would stop myself and do it right.

There are lots of people in the Work, but I don't want to see them. Sorry, but they are really not interesting. They are so boring. But they can come to me if they want to. Anybody who wants to can come and see me and talk to me and have a cup of tea. I'm a very sincere person. I never do anything I don't like. If I did really force something, you could see it on my face. I can't lie. The thing they said, that Luba only cooked for love — it is true.

If you are in the Work, what I understand about the Work and Mr. Gurdjieff's philosophy, you start at home. If your home is happy, then you can spread here, you can spread there.

I don't like hypocrisy. The hypocrisy makes me really sick. I hate snobbishness. I can be polite. I can be very ladylike when I want to. But I don't want to very often. Sorry, I don't. I think every person must have his own opinions, his own personality. And if you don't like me, you can lump it, as long as I don't hurt you. I don't hurt anybody. I'm happy. I can tell what I want to do, and nobody takes any bloody notice, because it's Luba talking. I used to yell from the kitchen, "You bloody things, if you're not happy, you can go somewhere else." People were delighted when I yelled at them. They always came back.

They would give me a kiss and bring me chocolates. When we came back from a holiday, after we were closed, we had five days to prepare everything, and the house was full of flowers, chocolates, plants, with notes: "We're so glad you're coming back. We miss you. Put this in your Bistro." Like a mother coming back to her children. I think that's life, and I don't care what other people think.

I'm never impolite; I'm always nice to people. I love people. I try to give them my best, to please them. What can I do more? Nothing.

There is nothing at Coombe Springs anymore. They took it all away. It is just housing. Idries Shah had it after Bennett. Beshara still has a little something there at Sherbourne, but I went, I couldn't find anything. Sherbourne was a beautiful place, a big castle. They did it up so nice. But when Bennett died, somebody else took it over, but they couldn't make a go of it.

After Bennett died, I was finished with them. I didn't want to see anybody. I thought, everybody is doing everything wrong. I thought, Why should I go there? If I talked to them, they thought I'm the cuckoo one. I remember two years after I left Coombe, when Bennett was still there, I went back to visit my friend Nottie — Olga de Nottbeck. She was a nice old lady. I left the Bistro; I said I was going to drive to Coombe, to see all my friends. It was tea time when I got there and they were all sitting around on their bottoms, the legs all cross.

I said, "Hey, everybody — anybody knows where is Nottie?" It was as if nobody was there. Nobody even looked at me. They were all concentrating, or constipated — I don't know what they were. Just sitting there. I started clapping my hands, shouting, "Wakey, Wakey!" One of the boys said, "Are you looking for somebody?" I said, "Yes. Nottie." "Oh, she must be in her hut." (That's what they used to call the rooms.) I said, "Thank you, very much. I am sorry to wake you all up." And I left.

They were all new students; they didn't know what's what. Then Mr. Bennett came in: "Luba, darling, how nice to see you," and all. You know how it is. He gave me a hug; he gave me a kiss. I said, "I'm sorry, Mr. B. I woke them all up in there." "It's all right, Luba. You don't have to worry about that."

I finally met Nottie, and I wondered if we could have a cup of tea. Nobody did anything. Why should we do anything for her? Then Mr. Bennett said, "You lazy things! Go and fetch a cup of tea for Luba. You know, she is Mr. Gurdjieff's niece." Well, that did it. Everybody jumps up and is making tea. I said, "I only want one cup of tea!"

When Bennett died everything was changed. The teaching was not the same. The teaching became more like slave driving. You came to Work, people were reading a little bit of Bennett books, a little bit of Gurdjieff books, but there was no teaching. It was all copying. Copying from other people.

Now, Work day makes sense when you need something done. Physical work is nice; with friends — see things get done.

I think all the trouble starts when Uncle died. They took what they could from him. Sometimes you get the impression you don't know if you're going up or down. People start doing their own things. You can read, but once you read, how do you go forward? You know what I mean? That's what happened with Mr. Gurdjieff's teaching. He went for twenty years, and after that it was finished. It was repeats all the time. New people would come, and it was repeated again. It would get badder and badder. It was like a story where somebody tells somebody who tells somebody else. And in the end, it is not the same story at all. That's what happened. That is my idea, I know, and I'm sticking to it.

The Movements are *fantastic*. They are very good. But you don't need a group; you don't need anybody there. You have the records, you do the Movements.

I always used to be in the front row in Movements; I was so good at them. It was first a special children's class. There was always a children's class — children first, grown-ups after. I don't even remember when I started Movements; I was very little. I remember people shouting at me, "No, no, no. Go this way, like this . . ."

You know, I never thought about it as anything special; it was just what we did; a part of life. We did Movements every day, every afternoon, for years. My mother was playing the piano; Mr. de Hartmann used to play the violin. Sometimes I didn't want to go; I used to hide myself. Then I would come and my Uncle would give me a dirty look. But he would never force anybody to do things. He never forced you to do Movements. I liked it most of the time. I loved the Movements themselves. I love dancing. I was always a mad dancer. It was dancing, and expressing myself. And then when I was asked to use my head along with it, it was a little more difficult. But I got it. I loved the dervish movements. Oh, I loved that! I put all my energy in them. We used to go round and round and round. I lasted longer than anybody else; they were dropping dead on the ground.

One thing my Uncle had was this Stop exercise. You are doing movements, going round and round, and then suddenly, "STOP!" We were always trying to get to the best position, not to fall down or to be on my knees — to be comfortable. Oh, it was funny.

Tom and Fritz Peters with two of
our Prieuré lambs

My father coming home in his
big car. Looks nice no?

This is J. G. Bennett. He helped
me a lot. I am godmother to his
son George.

I'm rolling up piroshky in the kitchen.

This is what my bistro looked like. I wish I had a better picture to show you.

The staff and me — we worked so hard in the Bistro, but we had fun too.

LUBA'S BISTRO

$\mathcal{M}$ r. $\mathcal{B}$ ennett said my cooking was not good enough for English people, so I took on a chef for that first restaurant. I was thirty-five years old and I had never made a business before. It was a more or less posh thing, you know. It was called Chez Luba. Then the chef made some deal with the man who gave me the money to start it and they put me out. But a friend of mine had a little cafe next to the restaurant in Mossop Street. She used to do lunches only, and she said, "Luba, why don't you come and start a bistro in the evening? I do my work at lunch and leave, and you can do your restaurant. I'll give you three months' rent free."

We started that restaurant with ten pounds! We didn't have anything. We didn't have any glasses. We didn't have any forks. I borrow from her and I start doing my cooking. My friends Peter Davis and Helen Cordet, the singer, used to come every night. There was pub next to me and she used to go into the pub and say, "Oh, I just had a wonderful dinner next door. Have you ever been?" And people start coming and coming. It was really very *fantastic*. After a fortnight, there were so many people, and I used to ask the customers, "Will you please bring glasses and forks?" We used to have such a wonderful collection — all kinds of glasses, all kinds of cups, all kinds of forks. My husband used to serve and wash up and I used to cook and serve.

We finally had to hire someone to do the washing up, and then we hired a woman, an Indian lady, who stayed with me thirty-five years, helping in the kitchen, then some waitresses. But the lady who gave us the free rent said, "I'm fed up with you. You're making more money than I am. Will you please go?" So we left again.

By now we have maybe six hundred pounds. One day we were driving around in our old car and we went to Yeoman's Row, just a little side street off the Brompton Road, and I saw a workingman's cafe and I said, "There. That is my dream." So we went and had lunch there. Two old ladies and a gentleman owned the place and they had no interest in selling. They said it was a good income. But we went again. And we talked again. Three times — and suddenly they say, "All right; we'll sell it." But they want two thousand pounds. You know, that's a lot of money in those times, two thousand pounds.

I said, "What are we going to do? We've got to do something." I was talking to our landlord at home. You know, he was only a workman, but he said, "Don't worry — I've got five hundred pounds in my Post Office account." A friend of mine said, "Don't worry, I've got a thousand pounds in my Post Office account." They all gave me the money and I started with that. When we knew we had to leave Mossop Street, I put a book by the door. I said, "I'm not staying here long. Maybe one day I'll have another restaurant. If you'd like to follow me, put your name and address here." And the customers, they all put their addresses. I had a good seven hundred. What we did, we sat down and we sent letters to everybody before we opened.

The first day opening, I couldn't move. They were all there. They were so happy that again we were having a bistro. They were giving me drinks and kisses and flowers and chocolate. It was *fantastic*. I felt like the Queen of Sheba. We started that way and we never stopped. This was all in 1960.

People were so happy in that place. They like the food, they like the decor. It was nothing, everything I used to hang on the walls: plates and onions and garlic. I used to go to Greece on holiday in the summer and buy plates and hang them up. People did my portrait and I hung it up. It all came like a mincing machine — you put it all in and it just comes out. And I started being stronger in myself, little by little. Because first I was so frightened. Will they like my food? Am I doing the right thing?

I knew I was a good cook, but some things I didn't know. I didn't know how to cook spaghetti in big quantities. Every time a customer ordered spaghetti I used to do it separately. Then one day somebody said, "What are you doing? You just cook it and put it in water in the fridge — you'll be all right." I learned. While I was working, I learned. I never took a class or anything in how to cook or how to run a restaurant.

At first we did everything by hand, chopping and mixing. After a while we got machines. The first was a potato peeler — you put in pounds of potatoes and it turns them over and over and rubs off the skins. One day I fill it up and start talking to somebody. Arthur comes in and says, "Why you have the potato machine on? There's no pota-toes in it." I say, "God, I put them in half an hour ago." Well they were there — very beautiful little tiny potatoes, all the same size.

My mother always cooked. You know how they are, being Oriental. Father comes home, everything must be there. He brings ten people, it'll be all right; she'll manage somehow. I was brought up in that kind of atmosphere. We always had people in the home. My mother was sitting there with a big, big table, with a big samovar and all the cakes. Anybody who comes has a cup of tea and the cakes. That was our way of doing it. The postman, the milkman, anybody — cup of tea. She was sitting there all day, after the Prieuré, serving cup of teas.

And I love cooking. When I cook and somebody eats, you give me a hundred dollars I wouldn't be so satisfied, because you are happy.

Nobody left that restaurant without saying, "Thank you, Madame Luba." It was ter-ribly enjoyable. I thought to myself, *mais*, there must be something cooking here. You know how you feel. People coming all the time, dropping in. If not eating, just come say, "Hello. You know I just drop in, Madame Luba, I ate already . . ." I say, "How dare you eat somewhere else?" "Oh, it was a party," excuses, that kind of thing. It was terribly, terri-bly happy and lovable. I mean, I'm only one person. Everything fell on me. I didn't know exactly how to do — you just create.

But I'm sure my family helped. You see, it was hard work, *mais* it was fun work. It was satisfying. Sometimes I used to sit down in my dining room and look out and say, "Thank you, God. Thank you, Uncle. Thank you, Mama." I didn't want anybody to be angry — they all helped!

It makes me happy even now to think of it. When I talk I get all excited, you know? I look at the photographs. There are some good ones to remember. Mrs. Wilkinson — she came to me one day and said, "I want to do something in my life." I say, "Well, why don't you come and be waitress?" She was fifty, maybe fifty-five this time. She was very skinny and very nice, *mais* very good for chucking people out. She used to come to the table where people making too much noise and *Bam!* with her hand on the table. "Be quiet, you young people!" The people say, "Who is she?" I say, "She's the chucker-off. She's in charge." They say, "I thought, Luba, you in charge." "No," I say. "She's in charge. She's much better than I am." She was very English and very British. She worked quite a bit. When I saw her the last time, this year, she said, "Luba, that was the best two years of my life."

There was so much life there. It was boiling. Sometimes I would say. "Oh, I can't manage it anymore; I'm tired." My body was tired. When I finished, I was sixty-five. Nobody would believe I was sixty-five.

It's not necessary to be old if you don't feel old. Your face gets old, but inside, if you've got life — why die before your time comes up? I can't understand that. People give up. Women don't do their hair; they don't dye their hair. I always had a manicure. I don't mean dressing up, but make yourself decent, smart.

I always said, if I had a hundred pounds, I spend a hundred pounds. If I had ten pounds, I spend ten pounds. If I don't have any, I don't spend any. I just sit and watch my television. That's life. I've had lots of money and I've had nothing. I lived like a princess in the Prieuré. We had everything we needed. My mother had a car; my father had a car; my Uncle had three cars. We lived, we worked, we suffered, but always we were alive. We were smiling.

I was so strong in those Bistro days — I was like a bull. I was fat. I was a big girl, then. Gosh, I was flying in those days. I used to wash my own lavatories at the Bistro. I hired someone; they didn't do it right, so I was back there doing it right. I remember once I was washing the pavement out in front with a hose and a brush. A young man came up and said, "I want to see the gov'nor." I say, "I'm the gov'nor." "Don't joke," he said to me. "What are you talking about? You're pulling my leg." "You go inside and ask," I said. So he did and somebody said, "She's the boss here." He was looking for a job and he couldn't imagine a boss cleaning her own pavement. I did that three times a week, every week. It was shining.

We never ate breakfast or lunch — we were picking all the time. We never had time to eat, except on Sunday. We always had the Sunday joint, the Yorkshire pudding, all that. Very English. It was really the only meal we had together. A lot of restaurants were open Sunday, closed Monday. I never was open on Sunday; I think Sunday is a rest day. When the staff have children, things like that, you can't have them sacrifice their lives completely.

My best day was always Saturday — the children's day. That was the funniest part. I used to go to the shops to see what I could buy for them. I used to buy teddy bears. You know, it just got started. Somebody came and brought children and I said, "You know, Saturday lunch is all children's day, if anybody wants to bring their children" — because lots of restaurants they don't want children in them. And it just started happening. Ice cream was on the house. I had lollipops and chocolates. I used to buy so many lollipops. The children used to come into the kitchen, "I haven't had one. I haven't had one." It wasn't really the lollipops, you know. They liked how I was paying attention to them, treating them like real people.

I remember once two Americans came and there were children running everywhere. The lady says, "Oh, God, what a noise." And she called me and said, "Madame, it's too much noise. We can't eat." And I say, "I'm very sorry, Madame, but this is Children Day and if you don't like it, you go." "But I don't like children," she says. I say, "Madame, I'm very, very sorry for you." And the husband, poor miserable man was sitting there, and he just sigh and look up. Anyway, they eat very quickly and they left, and she said, "I'm not coming back." I said, "Well, good luck to you." Who wants a customer like that? They don't like children, they don't like nothing.

There is always noise in a bistro. It was always something happening. People just came, they ate, they were happy, they were singing, guitar was playing. At first, I put my Russian music in there, but I stopped, because why should I spoil my records for them? Nobody can hear anyway. Then Tim came. That was what he was called then — not Reshad Feild — just Tim. He used to play and collect the money on a little plate. He sang, not Russian songs, but all these ballads.

Then I had another man, he used to be a ballet dancer but he got too old to be dancer and he started playing. His wife was ballet dancer too; she used to wait on tables. I always had people come to work who wanted to study something. My three washer-ups was studying for becoming doctors and one lawyer. They worked in the evening and studied in the daytime. They were good people who needed the work. I never took somebody who just said, "Well, I want to work . . ." I always wanted to know who I am taking. I had three postmen later who used to finish their jobs at twelve and then come and wash up from lunch until four.

I never had to fire anybody — no, one time I had to let somebody go. I took a chef because I thought, you know, he can do a little bit and we have a little bit rest. But when too many people came in the restaurant, he couldn't make so many things good at the same time. The pork chops was getting burned, the chips was not pretty, the decoration was not on the plate.

Me — you see what I done to the customers. I said, "It's not ready. You want to wait, you wait. If not, you can go." If something was running short, it took me maybe half an hour to make it. The rest of it was very fast service. Sometime I could hear them taking order — before they finish it's *Bam!* "Supreme Ready!"

Poor man — he didn't know he was coming or going. *Mais* if I don't have more white sauce or anything like that, I say, "I don't have any more sauce. You wait, or you like something else?" But to make what I need, always the onions had to be chopped, the peppers cut, things like that. So many little jobs. My mother used to come and sit couple hours and help. It was all ready. You see, I'm a very practical woman. If I'm lazy, then I'm lazy — nobody can move me. If I'm doing something, then I do it. You know, it's like that.

I had something in life. Some people work all their life and they die poor because they are so frightened. They never see anything. Nothing. It is so sad. If you work hard, you should play hard. I don't mean anyone should do the silly things I did. I gave lots of money away. But even that doesn't matter. If I could help somebody, it's worth it. It's worth it.

You know, it's funny — in the Bistro, people never asked for anything special. "What have you got, Madame Luba?" We never had a beer and wine license because the building was owned by the church. But we never charged for people if they wanted to bring in their own wine. Of course, then they stay longer. But what we had was a bistro, not a restaurant. A bistro and a restaurant are two different things. *Bistro* — that's Russian. When the cavalry officers used to come into the town, they used to rush into some inn, something like that, and say, "Bistro, bistro" — "quick, quick" — to eat fast and get back to their men. In a bistro you come, you eat, and you bugger off. That's the slogan. I used to say that. In English, not French. People used to say, "Oh, Luba, your English is improving!" "I know. Bugger off. That's English."

I talked to people when I was cooking. Oh, yes — I was the personality. "How are you, darling? Are you all right today, darling?" People would just come in the kitchen. You see, it was just a big square: half was kitchen and half was dining room. They could see me cooking. If people want a steak, I could say, "You go see what steak you want." They would open the fridge, choose their steak and bring it to me. That kind of thing. It was like a big family. Of course, sometimes I was so busy I couldn't talk to them. But sometimes instead of trying to explain the menu, the waitress would bring them in the kitchen to see exactly what was *galubtzy* or *pojarsky.*

All the restaurateurs in Brompton Road used to come around to see why the Bistro was working, why I am always full up. They used to come by and stare in the window. Then in August, when the Bistro was closed, they used to come over and pin their own menus up on the windows with directions how to get there.

We used to go to the opera sometime on Sundays. First we would do the food preparation for Monday, then I would start cleaning and polishing and everything else. We never really had any rest, only in August. We closed just like the French do. It's good to work very hard, but you must have some relaxation. That was always my principle: close in August and go away. One day to pack up, the second day we took the car and we left. We visited all the countries we could manage and then I lived like a queen. The best hotels, the best food, the best car. I always had a big car. I'm mad about cars.

To close in August was good for the business, too. We would go out and the dining room was painted, the kitchen was cleaned, everything was beautifully clean when we came back. I'm a fussy one; everything must be very clean.

The health inspectors would come to look. They look into everything, and they couldn't find anything wrong. They left me alone for a few years, and then they came again. It was a very nasty man. He opened all my ovens, but every Sunday the gas men used to come and clean them — burn them off, they called it — so the stove was always clean. Then he found the sink. Just the day before, Arthur had bought two sinks to replace my big one on the next Sunday, because the old sink was a little breaking. I said, "Don't worry, here it is. I got a new sink." And I showed it to him. Next thing I know he comes back to dinner, he and his helper and two ladies, and he says, "This is the cleanest restaurant in London. I never catch them doing anything dirty." That was so nice for me.

The dining room was so cozy. I loved it. We didn't usually put flowers on the table because the tables were quite narrow and they already had candles, the sugar, the salt.

The restaurant didn't look any different at lunch and at dinner, except at night it was dark with candlelight. Only the kitchen was lit up. I used to buy Chianti bottles to put my candles in. I would burn different colored candles. It was like a colored waterfall. People would break off little bits of them and I would shout from the kitchen, "Leave my blooming candles alone; I'm trying to make it pretty!" "Sorry, Madame." It's funny — I do the same thing myself with a candle on the table.

One thing I always like to do was present the dishes pretty. We put everything on the plate in the kitchen and the plate goes out: a little watercress there, the tomatoes there. I had all these little parts prepared in the morning, always to make it pretty. I didn't get that from my Uncle. His cooking was, you know, rough cooking. But my mother always used to make the food look so nice, even at the Prieuré. My Uncle used to say, "Bravo, Anna! Beautiful!"

But people used to pinch things from the Bistro. When I went to Russia I got little Russian ashtrays. In a week's time, they all disappear. When we went to France, I would pinch ashtrays from the restaurants there and use them. We stopped at a bistro-style place coming back once and I said, "I've been pinching ashtrays everywhere — could I pinch one of yours?" She was so charmed she gave me about thirty of them.

There was a man who made ashtrays out of clay that said Luba's Bistro. "Make me a few," I said. That was worse. They flew out of there. People used to ask for my autograph. They would pinch my ashtray and ask me to sign that thing! The Russian tea we served in a glass. I had those little silver glass holders from Russia, but they were all pinched. So I ordered some plastic ones. Those, they didn't pinch.

Not many people pinched menus. They would ask me first, especially Americans. "Please, can I have one?" and I would sign it for them. I had lots of caricatures. People would draw me. Even those they would pinch. But there's nothing you can do when you run a business like that. You expect to have to lose things. People would even pinch plates — just an ordinary plate, not a nice plate. One man paid the bill and then it was all gone: the plate, the knife, the fork, and the glass. All gone.

But it's one thing to cook and another thing is doing the business. At the start, my first husband took care of the books, the laundry, but when he left, Arthur came to help me, especially with the books. Arthur was a very good cook, too, and he started cooking everything, so I had more freedom. Imagine — we used to go there eight o'clock in the morning and never go out until three o'clock in the morning. I used to take all the staff home. You know, after midnight there are no buses. I couldn't afford to pay for taxis for everyone, so I used to drive them all around London.

Then we used to go to the clubs and dance in the early morning. Sometime I had a police escort home. All the Chelsea police knew me. They would say, "What are you doing out so late, Madame Luba. You're not drunk, are you?" "No," I say. I never drink much — a glass of champagne." "All right," they say, "we'll take you home." Oh, it was such fun.

I had such good workers. They used to come in at six o'clock; they eat a good meal, anything they want, then they put on their apron and start working. A few times I hired Chinese — they were *fantastic*. I could leave them in the dining room and just go out.

It was hard work. It was really hard work. When I get home, three o'clock in the morning, I used to find Arthur asleep in his chair. He says, "I can't move anymore." But you take a shower, you go to bed, and next morning you start all over. The last five, six years Arthur used to go in the morning and do lunch. I came in about three in the afternoon and take over. We didn't see each other that much for years! It was, "Hello, darling? How are you, darling?" He goes upstairs, I go downstairs.

Tim Field (Reshad Feild)
— so handsome with hair

My husband, Arthur, and me in
London, looking very posh

PEOPLE

One day I was very busy, and six young people came into the Bistro. You see, I could seat about forty-five people, squeezed down. We didn't have separate tables — we had long ones. You just sit wherever you could find a chair. One summer, Arthur built a place for the dustbin, you know, with doors, and I covered it with red linoleum to make it nice and clean and put flowers on it. Some people used to take their plates and eat standing there, like at a bar. On one wall I had a big hat from Spain hanging there — decoration, you know.

This day I was cooking, frying — I don't know what all I was doing — suddenly my waitress came to me and said, "Madame Luba, something very bad is happening." "What is it?" She said that they took down that Spanish hat. One of them put it on his head, and now they are putting spaghetti around it. I went there and I look at them. It was one of my regular customers, a very young man, who brought the other people in. I said, "What is all that? What do you think, I'm running a pigsty here? You behave yourself, or I'll call the police, or I'll put you out!"

The young man, he said, "Oh, Luba, you know who this is?" I said, "I don't care who it is. He is putting spaghetti on my hat. Who is it?" He said, "It's the Duke of Kent." I said, "I don't care who he is." So I went over to the Duke of Kent and I said, "I know your mother." "How could you know my mother?" he says. "Never mind," I said. "I know your mother, so listen to me. I'm giving you a bucket of water and a cloth. You clean up all that around you. Clean it all up."

I don't know — it was my personality, but they all clean it up. Then he took my hand, this tall, skinny guy, and said, "Madame Luba, I'm sorry. Can I come back?" I said, "You bloody well behave like that, you're not coming back. Now leave me alone, I'm busy."

His mother, Princess Marina, used to come nearly every week with her lady-in-waiting to have some peace and quiet. She used to love coming. She would speak to me in Russian. "Luba, darling, I love coming here; it is a place I can relax." I was so pleased.

I didn't care who that man was. Royal or anyone. My customers come to eat, and he was making a fool of himself. With my Spanish hat. I don't care if he is the Duke of Kent or the Queen of Sheba. You can't do that in my restaurant. He came back a few times. And he behaved himself. Then he got married. When they get married, it's finished up with me. The wives don't let them go out with their friends.

One of my regular customers was Tony Armstrong-Jones. He used to come in as a young man, with his father and mother. He had lots of travels he would talk about. For a while he used to come in nearly every day. And then one day I heard he was getting married — to Princess Margaret. I got mad at him. "You're getting married to Princess Margaret and you don't even tell your Auntie Luba?" He was all apologetic. It wasn't official until now and they didn't want people talking. I said, "Good luck to you." I said, "Be careful, Tony. She's a hard woman." He said, "How do you know?" I said, "Don't worry. I know."

Three or four years later, he came in about nine o'clock and said, "Princess Margaret is outside. She'd like to come in and eat, but she doesn't want to stand around." I said, "Tony, you go and wait in the car. When I have a table, I'll send someone out to get you. If she doesn't want to come in, she doesn't want to come in." A friend of mine was sitting at the table, in the corner. Friends used to come in and just sit and stay and talk. I told him, "Now listen. I got somebody waiting for a table, so if you want more coffee, come in the kitchen."

She comes in and says, "What is this place?" He tells her, "Well, I had all my childhood here. Here is Madame Luba." He told me to call her, "Ma'am." I said I would call her anything he wants; I don't care. The Princess seemed to relax once she got settled in, asking all kinds of questions about the place. She said she was very happy, and would be coming back, but we didn't see her again. But he always came back. He was a nice boy. Even now, he sees me in the street, he stops me, "Hi, Luba, darling." He was a good friend. I knew him when he was broke, you see.

There were always these lords and ladies coming. I don't remember their names. I never knew the names; I didn't want to know. You see, for me whoever they were, they were just people who come to eat. Hungry people. Of course, people would call, and say, "My name is Lord So-and-so, and I must have a table at such and such a time." I would say, "I'm very sorry, sir, but you must do like everybody else."

Nobody ever went hungry from the Bistro. I would serve four *galubtzy* on one plate — can you imagine that? — with the rice, and this lovely red sauce, and cream on top, and then you had borsch and some *piroshki* before. You can't eat more; you must be an elephant! People didn't take food from the Bistro. They finished what was on their plates — no doggy bags. I used to have a friend — he would come and order three chicken curries. First one, then another, then another chicken curry. I don't know where he put it. It wasn't that he ate only once a week — he was a very rich man. He just liked my food.

I had many friends. They were not customers any more — they were friends. That was the trouble. You can't charge your friends. They used to fight to pay me. I was ashamed to accept. You know, if you're invited to somebody's place to eat, to their place in the country, then later they come to the Bistro — how can you charge them? I couldn't bring them home because I had no time. Arthur would always say to me, "You've got too many friends, my love." I would say, "I can't help it. I have too many friends or I have no friends at all."

You know the Spanish painter — he was nutty and then suddenly he did the Queen's painting and he became very famous. He was a dirty old bugger. He used to come every day to the Bistro, and he was painting on my tables and on the napkins. I would say, "What are you doing, dirtying all my tablecloths?" I used to throw them in the dustbin. Then one day somebody came and said, "You should save them, you would have a fortune. He will become very known." But I would just wash them, try to get my tablecloths clean. He said to me, "You know, one day your tablecloths will be very expensive." I said, "I know. It's expensive now!"

Maybe I'm stupid, but when somebody well known comes, people get all excited. I never got excited. I was glad they came, I was glad to meet them. I was very proud they came, but they were just human beings for me.

I had lots of artists, actors. They had a studio nearby where they used to rehearse and they used to come for lunch with all their makeup on. The other customers would leave them alone. That was my law. I didn't want them bothered for autographs or anything.

When I would see a customer looking at one of these people I would say, "Leave them alone. They came for dinner. They want to relax." That was it. Whoever came, if it was the Queen of Sheba or any ordinary person, they eat, they relax, they have a good time.

If people stay too long, two, three hours, talking, and people are queuing, I would say, "Excuse me, could you please pay the bill? Other people would like to eat." I remember once with Tim — he is now called Reshad Feild, but his name then was Tim Field; Richard Timothy Field. We called him Tim. That was his name. He sang and he played guitar for the money. He had hair then — he was very handsome. All the waitresses, everybody liked him. He had a lovely smile. I liked him. I always liked him. He worked in the Bistro nearly two years. He made a record of a song he wrote for me. He called it, "Luba's Place." I still have it.

First when he left the Bistro, I didn't see him for at least ten years — more. Then suddenly I heard afterwards what he's doing. Someone came in from America, someone who said they were one of his pupils. She said, "You know, Tim Field. You know what he's doing now?" I said, "No. Not Tim. Oh, that silly bugger." "Yes," she said, "He's a big man in America." "Oh, I didn't know that. Good luck to him." What can you say?

Then one day he arrive and he was talk, talk, talk. He say, "Come on, I want to talk to you." I say, "All right, darling. You sit down, I come." I had half an hour. And only thing he done is talk. I say, "I thought you going to come ask me something. You talking all the time." Anyway, he talked, he talked. "What you think, Luba; what you think about . . ." And I gave him my opinion. And he left.

Then one time later he came with some of his people. They sat down, they order, and next thing my waiter come and say, "That party — they're not eating. People are queuing; the dining room is nearly full." I start shouting at him. I called him Tim. I said, "Your bloody philosophy, we don't want it here. When you come here, you eat. Don't spoil my atmosphere." I said, "You want to eat the spaghetti, or not?" Because I shout at him, his people — they all start shaking. They thought I was mad. How can I shout at him? He said, "Oh, I'm sorry, Luba, I forgot myself." I said, "Don't say that; not when you are sitting there with your pupils." I said, "I need the table. If you don't want to eat, then you get up. You should keep your eyes open. Look, there are people queuing. You've been here nearly two hours, and you haven't touched the bloody spaghetti!" Anyway, they all start eating very quickly. He talks and talks and talks and the food sits there.

You know, when he was working there, he didn't know who I was. Then maybe ten years after, someone said to him, "Do you know Luba's Bistro in London? Do you know that's Luba who is Mr. Gurdjieff's niece?" He nearly dropped dead. He didn't know.

But my customers were never rude. They were always very understanding. They behaved like they were in a private house. It was the welcome. I welcome all my customers. If I was in the kitchen, "Hi, hi, sit down, I'll see you later." I was always with them, wherever I was. There was always life. Life was there. It worked for me, because I have so much life. And they were happy there. It was nice. They loved me, too. It was a funny place. I still miss it. I miss the noise. I miss the people coming.

Still, I know I can't do it now. My body is too tired. I saw two, three hundred people a day, and they were all friendly people. You know, you work in most restaurants, you don't really see your customers. But I was always in the middle, "Luba, come have a glass of wine. Luba, come have a cup of coffee." Luba this, Luba that. It was always Luba. Even on the street, people would point and say, "That's Madame Luba." What is this? I haven't done anything.

But I made them laugh. I made them happy. Young people used to get engaged, they were poor, I would go in back and say, "Let's see, what do you need?" It was like a big family. I always thought God never gave me children because I had so many children around me. I was more of a mother than their own mother.

When I sold the Bistro, there was no announcement. I just disappeared. It was better that way. I just wasn't there. People would say, "Where is Luba?" The new owners would say, "Oh, Luba is tired. Luba is on holiday." After a couple of months, they would realize I'm no longer coming there.

My husband, Arthur, says if I had my way I would have given it all away. He says I served more free meals than anyone he ever heard of. But there were all these out of work actors. They used to come and say, "I got no money, Madame Luba." I would say, "Sit down, sit down. Eat." I used to have one, thirty years ago now, his name was Bruce. He was an artist, a painter. His grandmother left him about three thousand pounds. Little by little he lost it all. He came into the Bistro every day for twenty-five years, at six o'clock. He kept getting dirtier and dirtier, his suit, his shoes, everything else. I fed him for twenty-five years. Then he got mad at me. "Why do you close on Sunday, Madame Luba? I've got nowhere to go?" After dinner I would give him a cigarette, a shilling to buy a chocolate bar. I kept him going for twenty five-years.

One day, three young men came. It was so sad. They were very, very hungry. They were studying the menu and I could see they were choosing the cheapest thing they could manage. I asked them, and they said they had only a couple of shillings. All right, I said, I'll fix you something. So I gave them borsch and *piroshki*, and then some nice sweets. They thought, what a meal for two shillings! And they tried to give me the money. I said, "No, you keep the money. You can buy a cup of coffee somewhere." They went out, but they are looking over their shoulder as they walked, thinking I would come running after them. They couldn't believe it. But for my heart, it was so good. Things like that happened very often.

I don't understand people who borrow and don't return. I just can't understand people like that. Sometimes it takes a long time, though . . . There was one very nice, very gentle young man. He came to me and said, "Madame Luba, I must go now to some far countries to make some money. Can you lend me sixty pounds?" That was lot; it was like asking for a month's pay. Anyway, I lent him that sixty, and I didn't see or hear from him for four years. I thought about him. Where's my sixty pounds? Gone. He never knew I had those thoughts. He was always good-hearted, too. He knew what he would do. Suddenly he arrived, all dressed up, a beautiful car. He said, "Luba, darling, here is your sixty pounds, and another forty pounds for you." "What do I need the forty?" I said. "I am so glad to get my sixty back!"

Sometimes friends, they were the worst. Customers we hardly knew, I help them out and they would repay. But some friends really took me for a ride. They really took advantage of me. You work hard for thirty years, and there isn't much to show for it. Never mind. I was happy. Isn't that the important thing? Happiness and health come first.

LUBA'S LAMENT

Luba Stood at the Golden Gate
Her Voice Was Sweet and low
She meekly asked the man her fate
And where She ought to go!

"What have You done Luba" St. Peter asked
"to Seek admission here?"
"I Kept a Bistro down below
For many and many a Year."

St. Peter opened wide the gate
And gently pushed the bell
"Come Inside Luba and Choose Your Harp
You've had Your Share of hell!"

This was a present from a friend who understood how
much hard work it took to make things run smoothly.

Stonehenge was wonderful.
So many big rocks!

When I'm at Disneyland,
I'm just like a kid again.

I love convertibles!

TRAVELS

I would like to go back to visit Greece, the islands. When I first went to Athens it was all little houses. Last time we stayed in Athens, it was terrible. It was like New York. I couldn't recognize it. The first time I was in Athens I had a convertible, a blue one. That was when I was first with my husband, Arthur. At that time no women drove in Athens. Now everybody drives, *mais* before, when the Greeks saw me in my convertible everybody was whistling. They used to chase me around. Oh, it was so fun.

My cousin, Dushka, the singer, came from America that summer. We were on the beach one day when Arthur was someplace else, and all the young men came around because they thought, you know, rich English girls. We were dressed very nicely. And we gave twelve young men the same rendezvous in the same cafe, at the same hour, for coffee. I knew we were going to pass that time by that cafe to go somewhere else to have dinner. And we drove by and they were all sitting there. Nobody knew each other. And then I came very near and I say, "Ooooo woooo!" And they all get up — they think I call them. And I went CHOOOO and drive away fast. Arthur says, "You are a naughty girl." I used to love making funny, funny things. It makes all the difference in life, no? Little bit mischief here and there.

But I love the Greek islands. They are so beautiful — so clear, so clean. You go to church on Sunday, it is all so clean. I remember we went to this tiny little island, only maybe ten houses and a church and an old monastery. The treasure in that church was *fantastic*. There was only one taxi; everybody is going on donkeys' backs. I said I'm not riding on a donkey's back. When everybody left, I had the taxi come back. I started praying, with the candles. There were two priests there — they were so surprised. They said it was the first time they saw somebody come back to pray. The tourists just come in and go out. I said, "Well, I always would pray in a church." I don't remember the name of the church, but it was very, very old.

My Uncle never taught us religion. I went to church with my mother and my grandmother. My Uncle, the others — they went to church at Easter, Christmas, the times you're supposed to go. But my Uncle never taught us how to go to church, or pray, or anything like that. And he never liked the priests or the nuns. When we were out driving and he saw a priest, he would say, "Shoo! Son of a bitch."

I was always frightened he would discover I was going to church every Sunday morning. One Sunday morning in Paris I was coming out of the church near two shops where he used always to go to buy something and he saw me. I was frightened — what would happen? He said, "Good girls. Good girls. You think I didn't know you were going to church? I knew. Good girls. You should do what you want. You want to go to church? You go to church." He never went to church like that, but I know he believed. I was so relieved that day. Afterwards, he used to ask me, "Did you go to church?" "Yes, Uncle." "Thank God," he says, "there's something good." In London I go to hear the Metropolitan Anthony, Father Anthony Bloom. He was a doctor and then he became a priest. He married me — I think it was his first wedding. He is a very unusual man.

And I'm a practical old girl. I've been all my life a practical old girl. All my life I worked with my hands — I'm not an intellectual. But somehow I tuned up and went forwards and forwards. I used to say, "You come to me if you want to ask very simple questions, things I know. Because I won't tell you if I don't know; I don't feel it." I'm not one who can brush your head with all this wind. If I had experience, if I knew it, I would tell you.

They ask, when I die, what am I going to be? How far am I going to fly away? I say, "I don't know. Anybody who flies never came back. It must be good there." I mean, you don't ask Luba that thing. Luba is a practical woman. I can do things simply. The complicated way is not my way.

Lots of people come, and they are quite happy; they come back. One young man, he came back three times. "Can I come back tomorrow?" I said, "You can come every day. Come tomorrow for lunch." He was so happy; he said he would bring me a big bunch of flowers. I said, "Don't bring the flowers. I know you haven't got any money." And I gave him ten pounds. "What is that for?" "That's from Luba." He took it, and he was happy. I knew he was starving, poor man. Arthur is saying to me, "Look, if you're going to go and do that, *we're* going to be starving."

But really, we are so blasé with our little luxuries when you think about it deep down. Water is there, hot water is there, gas is there. I think we get used to all these luxuries and we have big evils in life. How we take for granted. I make myself never feel blasé about today's luxuries because today you are blasé and tomorrow you can fall on your head and you've had it. You know what I mean — every little thing, it gives me pleasure.

I love cars. Every few years I see a lovely car and I say, "Can I have that one?" You know, I've been paying for my cars for more than thirty years — I always exchange them. I always had convertibles, big cars. I'm a mad driver. I love it. On my first trip to America, we toured California in a car. In San Francisco they gave me an automatic shift. I never drove that in my life before. I was all right on the road, but we came into the city and every time we came to a red light it was terrible, because I couldn't find the bloody clutch. I never used the car in San Francisco. But I liked the food in America. I thought it was very good, especially the salads. I liked Fisherman's Wharf — all that fresh fish and the crabs. What I really liked in America was the pancakes in the morning, with syrup. I ate them nearly every morning. In the excitement of traveling I lose weight. I lost weight in America, and I ate like a pig. I didn't want to miss anything!

I tell you about when I went to Ceylon. I been there five times. It is so interesting, because there is so much religion there. They are Buddhists, you know. And there are all these snakes around, the cobras. They don't touch them. You hear it, you just pause there. You don't look at them. They're all right.

In Ceylon everyone was eating with their fingers. I love eating with my hands if it's something solid — a good piece of chicken. I'm not clumsy, but there I just couldn't do it. They take a little rice, a little sauce — everything is so beautifully made. I was the only one many times in the party who had to have a fork and knife, but I always wanted to eat what the people eat, wherever we were. We went to Italy, we ate Italian. Went to Greece, we ate Greek. They would know in a restaurant I was not a native and they would try to give me "Continental" food and I would yell. When you go to a country, you want to taste that country. The only place I didn't like the food was Algeria — all we got was beans and mutton. But they had a beautiful, big beach. Very nice.

I went first to Ceylon because my doctor, Dr. Fonseka, was from there. We became very good friends and one year she asked me to go there with her. I said I would love to, so I went and I met everybody — Mrs. Bandaranike and Sir John, the ex-Prime Minister. He used to go there every summer; he was a nice old man. He really fell in love with me. We became very big friends together. Every time I went to Ceylon, I was received like a queen. They had two elephants they used to bring into the garden. It was so beautiful. They gave parties for me, and took me to parties.

My friend's son was getting married and they made a big party in the garden next to the house. There was a buffet. Everybody took a plate and filled it up so much you knew they couldn't eat it. They leave half. You know how these rich people are. About two hours later, everybody is sitting there and I realize, I look around, on the wall there were about forty kids sitting, all beggars, all ages. I went into the kitchen — there were five cooks — and I said to them, "Anything left?" "Oh yes. Madame." There was a big dish of pork chops. I took them to give to the kids, and five chickens and three big bowls of rice. And the kids all disappeared. Five minutes later, they came back. They had washed all the bowls and brought them back. Then I gave them some fruit.

Then someone came in the kitchen — you know how they are. "Servants! There's not enough food on the table." They said, "Madame, we haven't got any more." "What do you mean?" "This lady took it all."

I said, "Look at them, these pigs. They don't eat half of what they took." She said to me, "Are you happy, Luba?" "Yes." "Then that's all right." I was so happy. I could feed them all.

Sometimes I look behind me, at my life. There was quite big excitement in my life. It was something I had myself. No one else did it for me — you know what I mean. All these kids, all these people I met.

Another day we went picnicking in the mountains. Many of the Ceylonese people live in huts made from earth. I saw one very old man sitting there. We're all eating our lunch. A very dirty old lady came out from the hut and I thought, "Oh, gosh, they must be very poor, these people." I went in the hut. Beatrice was my host, and she said, "Luba, where are you going?" I said, "Mind your own business." I went in the hut. There were two little beds — nothing else. No food. The two skinny, very old people, sitting there. All white, curly hair. I remember it so well.

I came back to my picnic and said, "Now you stop eating." Beatrice said, "You're not going to give her our food, are you?" I said, "Yes. You're all too fat and too healthy. Come on." We didn't have any bowl, anything to give it to them in. I went back to the hut and I saw a big bowl and I took it. She was looking at me, the old lady, wondering what was happening. I didn't speak her language. I took that bowl and I put everything I could manage in it. Then I pinched a bottle of wine. Beatrice said, "They won't drink wine." I said, "Never mind."

I'll never forget that impression. I brought that big bowl with the food and I put it down in the lap of that woman and she stared at it. She didn't look at me; she stared at it. I was watching to see what she would do. She held the bowl up to her husband to smell, because he was blind. They started eating. Suddenly she realized what was happening, and she picked up two flowers, I don't know from where, and brought them to me. It was so touching. I was crying. I'm still crying.

It makes me so happy when I can do that. Really happy. All my soul is sighing with pleasure.

But also I love to travel. I used to be very adventurous. I wanted to taste everything.

In 1977 I went to Russia. I went with a group, you know, fourteen people together. We saw one museum, a church, another museum, another church. One day I said to the guide, "I've had it with your museums, your churches. You go where you want. I'm going by myself." So I'm walking, and I felt someone is following me. You know how you have this feeling? I turn around and there was a young man, not more than twenty. I didn't do anything. But the second day (I stayed two days by myself), I went again. And the same young man is there. So I go up to him and I say, in Russian, of course, "Why are you following me? Why don't you just come with me? We'll have a nice time together." He didn't know how to deal with that. So we went off together, to a nice café, a nice museum. We had lunch together and this poor young guy, he was always looking, looking. I said, "What are you looking at?" He said he was afraid they were watching him! It was so funny.

Afterwards, he explained he was a student who also worked for the government. He said, "You see, your name is Russian; your passport shows you were born in Russia; you go off by yourself, so they tell me to watch you." But we had a nice time. In the evening we went dancing.

I went to the Russian circus. When I came in they were already started and I could hear they were saying, "Come on, Luba. Come on, Luba." I thought they were talking to me — but it turns out that was the elephant's name! After the show I went backstage; I wanted to meet the elephant. I said to them, in Russian, "My name is Luba. Can I go and see the elephant?" They said, " Oh, yes, Madame."

I was in Red Square when they change the guard. It was something beautiful to look at. I was taking pictures. A friend said, "Oh, don't do that. You never know. A Russian officer is standing there." I went up to him and I said, "If I take some photographs, you think I'm going to be arrested?" He said, "No, Madame. Can I take one for you?" So I stand there, and he takes my picture.

My name is "love" in English. I always liked my name. There are not many people called Luba — even the Russian people have very few Lubas. There are Annas and Veras, Lidas, Zhenyas — but very few Lubas. Now probably lots of Olgas. Really it's *lubov* that's Russian for love — Luba is the diminutive. I used to love it in France when they would call me Lubov Dmitrieevna. I thought it was so great — kiss my hand. The English call me Lubu, all kinds of thing. They always used to call me Madame Luba. It's sort of like I was running a brothel, eh?

Now I think somebody could make a Bistro in many places in the world and it would be a good business: good food, everything always ready, big portions. I show you the menu we had and then I tell you a little more about what we did.

LUBAS BISTRO

ONION SOUP   -   LUBAS RUSSIAN
CORN ON THE COB   BORSCH
SALAD MIXED -   SOUP DU JOUR   -
PIROSHKI -   -   PÂTÉ   -   -   -
FRUIT JUICES (ORANGE, GRAPEFRUIT, PINEAPPLE, TOMATO)

SPECIALITY

SHACHLIK - -   -   -   -   -   -
BOEUF STROGANOFF - -   -   -   -   -
POJARSKY - -   -   -   -   -   -
LUBAS GALUBTZY - -   -   -   -   -
CRÊPE A LA REINE - -   -   -   -   -
CHICKEN SUPREME - -   -   -   -   -
CHICKEN CURRY & RICE - -   -   -   -
STUFFED GREEN PEPPERS - -   -   -   -
VOL-AU-VENT - -   -   -   -   -
BEEF CURRY & RICE - -   -   -   -   -
EGG CURRY & RICE - -   -   -   -   -
KOFTA CURRY & RICE - -   -   -   -
SPAGHETTI MAISON - -   -   -   -
SPAGHETTI WITH MEAT BALLS - -   -   -
LAMB CHOP GARNI - -   -   -   -
PORK CHOP GARNI - -   -   -   -
ENTRECÔTE STEAK GARNI - -   -   -
HOLSTEIN STEAK GARNI - -   -   -
TOURNEDOS STEAK GARNI (if you're lucky) - -   -

TRIFLE - -   -   ORANGE SALAD -
MERINGUE GLACE   CHEESE & BISCUITS
BANANA MELBA -   BREAD & BUTTER -
PEAR MELBA -   CHUTNEY -
PEACH MELBA -   COFFEE - -   -
ICES -   -   RUSSIAN TEA -
ICE & CHOCOLATE   YOGHOURT -
          SAUCE   COCA-COLA -
LUBAS SPECIAL   ORANGE SQUASH -
         CERNIC   LEMON SQUASH -

BRING YOUR OWN WINE — NO CORKAGE

Luba's Bistro menu

Recipes

$\mathcal{B}$ *istro cooking is to have everything ready* that you can so the food comes out of the kitchen very fast. Also it is to make a few things well, and to make different combinations of them for variety. On my menu we had *piroshki:* you cook the meat and you can use it for the filling, you can use the same meat for curry if you want — you can even use it for stroganoff if you got good meat and you want to make the dish cheaper. Then you have the pancake: you use the same kind of pancake for the *cernic,* and for Crêpe à la Reine. The sauce for Crêpe à la Reine is the same sauce you use for Chicken Supreme and for Vol-Au-Vent.

I won't put anything in this book that I didn't cook myself. This is what I made, what people like, and what I can cook. I can't say I'm a Cordon Bleu. I'm just a good cook; an ordinary good cook.

Another thing — I never made something if I could buy it better. I used to buy cans of tomato paste, the yoghourt we served, chutney, ice cream. Why should I spend my time doing something if somebody already does it well? Also, I used to use concentrated stock we could buy to add to water we cooked the beef or chicken in. It was very helpful.

Our menu at the Bistro stayed the same all the time. Because if I change something, then somebody comes especially to eat that and it isn't there and she would cry, "Where is it, Luba? What are you trying to do? Change your Bistro?"

Sometimes people would come to me and ask how I make something. But I never cooked from recipes at the Bistro. I never made these measurements the way it says in cookery books. I taste as I cook. That's how I know.

They asked me to go on the radio, but I refused. I didn't want to reveal all my secrets. You could go all around London, you couldn't find such cooking anywhere else. That's why I'm so proud, you see.

The food was always the same: the borsch, everything. I never changed the taste. Never. People were amazed. They came for thirty years and always the same things. In thirty years we only took two dishes off: *goulash* we took off because, first, the meat is very expensive and then, when you make it and you don't sell it one day, the next day it is not very good. The meat is cut in small pieces and by the next day it will be falling apart. Veal Blanquette, it was the same thing. One day and it's finished: you can't use it any more. And veal prices got very, very expensive. My prices were so low it was ridiculous.

At first we didn't know; we just guessed. We figured the cost of what went into it and then figured maybe twice that.

You see, my food it's not civilized food. It's food people eat when they're hungry. You go to Luba's Bistro to eat, not to be seen. Can't be — people are all crammed together at a long table, nobody can see how they're dressed.

But people made very few complaints. Maybe sometime the steak was a little bit tough, or they didn't like garlic in their food. I like garlic. People who were vegetarian, very strict, I didn't have much for them. I had rice, potatoes, salad.

One Saturday night somebody brought me some fresh corns. I said to the customers, "Who wants some?" They loved it. I just boiled it and put skewers in and lots of butter. But after that I didn't have any more fresh corn; I start buying it in these big tins. People liked that okay, too, so we had corn on the cob all the time. It was an appetizer. But I never made vegetables. Once or twice I put vegetables on the menu — nobody wanted it. If you do *haricot verts* or something, how would you serve it? Not with Galubtzy, not with green peppers.

Other starters we had, some was bought and some I made. Fruit juices I bought, of course. Pâté I used to buy, too. I tried making it, but I didn't like it. There are so many good French pâtés you can buy; why should I make it? It's only chopped liver. I would just serve it with a couple pieces of toast.

For the soups, you want a good stock. I used to take the beef I was planning to use for Piroshky, even for the beef curry, and put it in a pot well covered with water and bring to a boil and then simmer until it's tender. You take the meat out and keep it in the fridge until you need it. Add some beef bouillon cubes to the stock to make it more tasty and you have the starting for soups. Most of the time the *soup du jour* was barley soup, I give you that recipe. These are the soups and appetizers.

SOUPS & APPETIZERS

Onion Soup

2 tablespoons oil
4 tablespoons butter
4 pounds onions, sliced
2 quarts beef stock

1 tablespoon dried mint leaves
Salt and pepper to taste
8 slices toast
8 heaping tablespoons grated Gruyère
    or Cheddar cheese

Put the oil and butter in a skillet and heat gently until the butter is melted. Add the onions and cook until they turn golden brown. Transfer to a soup pot. Add the beef stock and mint. Bring to a boil, then simmer one hour. Add salt and pepper to taste.

To serve, use a bowl you can run under the broiler. Put the soup in the bowl, then float a slice of toast on the soup. Put the cheese on the toast and place the bowl under direct heat until the cheese is melted and begins to brown.

Luba's Russian Borsch

Makes Twelve Servings

There are forty-two kinds of borsch in Russia. I tell you, I have tasted lots of borschs, and nothing is better than mine. Everybody used to say, "How do you do this borsch, darling? It is fantastic." It was so rich, you see. The cream you put in at the end mixes with all the vegetables; it makes it so much softer and nice. You can use cream or you can use sour cream, if you like.

I learned to make this borsch from my mother. She was making it at the Prieuré. She was cooking it at my Uncle's flat. This blooming borsch comes from generations and generations! It makes a big pot of borsch.

2 large onions, sliced	3 6-ounce cans tomato paste
2 tablespoons butter	6 beef bouillon cubes
2 tablespoons oil	1 teaspoon dried mint leaves
1 large cabbage, chopped in small pieces	1 teaspoon dried tarragon leaves
2 pounds beets, peeled and shredded (small ones are better)	1 teaspoon salt
1 pound carrots, shredded	½ teaspoon pepper
	¾ cup heavy cream

Sauté the sliced onions in butter and oil in a skillet until they are golden brown. Transfer to à large soup pot.

Add the rest of the ingredients, plus three quarts of water. Bring to a boil and then simmer two hours.

When serving, float a tablespoon of heavy cream on the top.

Leftover soup can be strained and refrigerated for a delicious cold borsch.

Barley Soup

This was usually the Soup du Jour.

6 ounces pearl barley, rinsed
½ pound carrots
½ pound potatoes
3 large stalks celery
1 large onion, sliced
1 tablespoon butter

1 tablespoon oil
¾ pound stew beef, cut in small pieces
½ teaspoon dried mint leaves
½ teaspoon dried tarragon leaves
2 tablespoons chopped parsley
Salt and pepper to taste

Soak the barley for at least two hours (overnight is better).

Chop the carrots, potatoes, and celery. Leave good-sized pieces. This is not civilized food — it's like peasants' food. I like rough soups. Then you got something to chew. Set the vegetables aside.

Sauté the onion in the butter and oil until golden brown. Transfer to a soup pot. Add the beef, vegetables, five cups of water, the mint, tarragon, parsley,salt and pepper. Bring to a boil and simmer one hour, or until the beef is tender.

Unfortunately, you have to stir this from time to time when it's cooking, because the barley sticks on the bottom of the pot. It's heavy. It goes down, *capice?* You can't go off and watch television and forget it's cooking!

My mother used to say if you burn your soup, you put it carefully in a new pot and then you put in a good lump of charcoal you have rinsed off and let it simmer until the charcoal takes up the burned taste. Better not to burn it in the first place.

Piroshki

Makes about Sixteen Piroshki

Although we had piroshki listed with starters on the menu, lots of people from offices used to come into the Bistro for lunch and order piroshki and chips, or piroshki and salad. Cup of coffee and a sweet and they were very happy.

There are so many kinds of piroshki in Russia, in Poland, in Hungary. Some people make them with pie dough and bake them. This one is my own, and it is really good. If you cook the meat and then cool it, you can remove any fat remaining easily.

1½ pounds lean beef	1 teaspoon dried mint leaves
1 teaspoon salt, plus more to taste	Pepper to taste
2 tablespoons butter	One batch crêpes (recipe follows)
2 tablespoons oil	2 hard-boiled eggs, chopped very fine
2 large onions, minced	Oil for frying piroshki

The day before serving piroshki, trim any fat from the beef. Put the meat in a pot with enough water to cover it. Add a teaspoon of salt. Bring to a boil and then simmer for two hours, or until the meat tests tender when you poke it with a fork. Allow the beef to cool, then remove it from the liquid. and store, covered, in the fridge overnight or until well chilled. (Use the stock for making borsch!)

When the beef is chilled and you want to make the piroshki, heat the butter and oil together in a skillet over medium heat. Add the minced onions and sauté until golden brown. Meanwhile, mince the beef well. Do not use a food processor, as it will turn the beef into paste. Chop it up fine with a knife. Add to the browned onions. Add mint and stir. Add salt and pepper to taste and continue cooking and stirring for ten minutes. Set aside to cool.

Meanwhile, make the crêpes and let them cool slightly for ease of handling when you assemble the piroshki.

Put a heaping tablespoon of meat mixture in the middle of a crêpe. Top with chopped egg. Wrap the mixture in the crêpe, folding the sides in first and then bringing the top and bottom edges over. Repeat the procedure for the remaining crêpes, setting each one aside, smooth side up, while you assemble the rest. Letting them sit a few minutes like this will help them stay together during the next step.

Warm the oil in a skillet over medium heat; you want about one-quarter inch of oil covering the bottom of the pan. Fry the piroshki about 2 minutes on a side, until they are browned. Start cooking them smooth side up to help them stay folded.

Crêpes

We really used a lot of crêpes in the Bistro. We used to make three hundred of them a day! They were used for the piroshki, the Crêpe à la Reine, and for Luba's Special Cernic. You can make your crêpes a day ahead and keep them in the refrigerator, covered with a slightly damp cloth. You can make them two days ahead, but after that the edges start to curl and get hard.

1 cup all-purpose flour
1 cup self-raising flour (or substitute 2 cups of all-purpose flour plus 2½ teaspoons baking powder and a good pinch of salt)

¾ cup milk, plus up to ½ cup more if you've left the batter overnight
¾ cup water
2 eggs, beaten
2 tablespoon melted butter, to grease the crêpe pan

Mix the flours together in à large bowl. Add the milk and water and beat until smooth. Add the eggs and beat again until well blended. You want a batter that is a little thicker than crêpe batter usually is. Now let it sit: overnight in a fridge is best; one half-hour at room temperature is okay. You can make the crêpes immediately, but they are more fragile and easier to tear.

Use a small crêpe pan or skillet. Grease it between crêpes, using a pastry brush and melted butter. Make the pancakes thin (thin the batter if necessary with the extra milk) and stack them up as they are cooked. Cover them with a slightly damp cloth towel as you work.

Crêpes freeze very well. After they are cooled, put a piece of plastic wrap between each crêpe and they won't stick together. Wrap them and freeze them. You can remove just a few for a quick meal or a dessert.

Russian Salad

You can use this like zakuska — hors d'oeuvres. This is easy to do. You don't need to worry about amounts. Just put in what you like — a good mixture. Try to cut everything in little squares, about the same size, not big and lumpy.

Cook vegetables like these:

Potatoes	Carrots
Beets	Green beans
	Peas

You can also put in some vegetables you don't need to cook:

Onions	A little bit of celery (to make it crunchy)
Green onions	Chives, parsley, some fresh tarragon, if
Mushrooms	you have it

Mix all the vegetables and herbs together in à large bowl and toss with dressing to taste.

You can use the Bistro Dressing on (page 94), or a simple French dressing. Let it sit in the fridge for an hour or two, so the taste goes into the vegetables. You can add a spoon of mayonnaise before you serve it. It is very nice. It makes you hungry!

～

These were all the starters we used to have on the menu, but twice a year I used to give a party. I used to do all the food, the music was on, all our staff used to come and all our customers that I liked.

I remember the last time I invited seventy-five people and we finished by having two hundred. It was a Saturday and people would come to the door and see what was going on and say, "Oh, are you closed?" And I would say, "No, come in." I made so much food: Russian Salad and chicken and some very good hors d'oeuvres with eggs and mayonnaise. I would cut a piece of bread very thin and slice hard-boiled eggs very fine. I put one anchovy on it and a little mayonnaise and a bit of tomato or cucumber for decoration. When you make a big tray like that it is very beautiful. Very good to eat, too.

Russian Salad was very good, too. My Uncle used to like this kind of salad. I used to make it for him.

Mr. Gurdjieff's Special Salad

This salad seems to be famous all on its own. We had something like it lots of times — not for big occasions, but when somebody was coming, somebody new to impress, you know, my Uncle would say in a big whisper, "That is my salad."

He used to come into the kitchen sometime and make it himself. He was tasting all the time. Valya and I and my auntie used to cut, cut, cut, and give to him. Anything he didn't like he used to throw it on the floor. Oh, I used to be so angry! You clean that kitchen and it's shiny and then — *bang* — on the floor!

Then he says, "That's enough cut. You good girl. Make a big bowl like that." By the time I used to be finished and put it all in the fridge it was starting to get fermented. And the bloody people there really still eat it. I used to say, "It's finished!" "No, no, no — it's all right for the American and English. They don't know how to eat."

One day at Coombe Springs it was Mr. Bennett's birthday and he said, "You think you can make me Mr. Gurdjieff's salad?" I said, "With pleasure. Just give me the money and the car. I go and fetch everything I need, and I make you salad. It's easy." I made it, but it took the whole day.

And you can't have a recipe for it. It costs the earth! You put anything you can find in that thing: chopped tomatoes, cucumbers, radishes, celery, any vegetables you can find — only raw vegetables. No lettuce, because lettuce gets very soft. It used to have nuts in it; it used to have green olives you cut in pieces away from the stone; it used to have sometimes prunes in small pieces — it was like a dustbin. Chutney — he used to put lots of chutney. Sweet chutney that must be cut in small pieces, because chutney generally comes in nice big pieces. And he used to like those little green things in vinegar — capers. Twenty, thirty things used to go in that salad. Sometimes he would even put apples — any kind apples. I think he would put anything he could find in there.

There was always put in some tomato ketchup. I remember they used to bring it from England because we couldn't find any in Paris. And dressing he just put on a little bit vinegar and then some oil. You never do anything to it; just chew it. Oh, it's very easy to do.

Salad Mixed

Mostly what I made in the Bistro for mixed salad was cucumber, tomato, watercress and green onions, chopped and mixed together. You can use lettuce, you can use whatever else you like in salad. I used to use spinach sometimes. Sometimes somebody would ask for something special. The waiters would tell me what people want: "There is a gentleman who wants green peppers on his salad." All right; he'll get. (You know, peppers are something new in the world. I don't remember having them when I was a child. Little hot ones, yes, but not the big green one.)

Other simple salads I used to make were: cucumbers, sliced thin and dressed with two parts oil to one part lemon juice (salt & pepper to taste); and beets, shredded very fine, dressed with a simple French dressing and chilled.

The main thing about my salad was my dressing. People would come to the Bistro with a bottle and ask to have a little of my dressing. Why not? But now you can make it yourself.

Bistro Dressing
Makes about Four Cups

1 cup red wine vinegar
½ cup sugar
½ cup mustard (Dijon is best)
2 bay leaves
½ teaspoon dried mint leaves

¾ teaspoon dried tarragon leaves
1 lemon, diced
2 cups corn or olive oil
3 cloves garlic, crushed
1 teaspoon salt
½ teaspoon pepper

Put all the ingredients in a bottle and shake. This dressing is best if it's been sitting overnight, but it must sit at least two hours before you use it to let the flavors go together. Just make it up and leave it in the fridge for when you want it.

Aubergine Caviar

Makes Six to Eight Servings

What they call in America eggplant is called in London by its French name, aubergine.

This is another hors d'oeuvre I used to like to serve at parties. If you can get eggplants that are not too thick, you can just roast them over a gas flame. Otherwise you'll have to steam them, too. Here is the recipe.

1 pound eggplant (Japanese and Chinese varieties work well here)
2 cloves garlic, minced

¼ cup olive oil
1½ tablespoons wine vinegar
Salt and pepper to taste
Black olives (for decoration, if desired)

Poke the eggplant all over with a fork. Using a long kitchen fork, hold each one over a gas flame so that it burns and blackens the skin all over. If you are using Japanese or Chinese eggplant, squeeze it, to see if it's soft. When it is, hold it under cold running water and rub off all the blackened pieces. If you are using the larger American eggplant, you can't wait for it to soften. When it's blackened all over, rub and rinse it as above, then cut it into thick slices and steam it until it's soft.

Mash the eggplant with a fork. Add garlic, oil, vinegar, salt and pepper.

Chill. Decorate with black olives and serve with crackers or pita bread.

SPECIALTY

Shachlik

I used leg of lamb for my shachlik. I used to get four good-sized portions from one leg of lamb, but you could get five or six portions depending on the size of the lamb. If you can, get your butcher to bone it, telling him that you want good, big chunks. Some meat markets sell chunks of lamb for shish kebab. They may be okay, but I wouldn't buy them if they're small pieces.

Start this the day before you plan to serve shachlik.

1 leg of lamb
1 glove garlic, crushed
1 teaspoon curry powder
4 tablespoon wine vinegar
4 bay leaves
1 teaspoon dried mint leaves
1 teaspoon dried tarragon leaves
1 teaspoon salt
½ teaspoon pepper

1 cup corn oil
Garnish with some of the following, your choice:
plumped raisins
chopped cucumber
radishes
tomatoes
watercress
pitted prunes

The day before you plan to serve your shachlik, remove the meat from the bones and then trim off all the fat and gristle, if your butcher hasn't done it for you. Cut meat into cubes and put into à large bowl.

Your next step is to add all the rest of the ingredients *except* the oil and garnishes and mix it all together. You want to cover the meat mixture with oil next, and then it goes into the fridge to marinate. (You may want to put it into a smaller container.) Leave it for twenty-four hours if possible, or at least overnight.

Place lamb on skewers and cook under broiler, turning frequently.

Serve on a bed of rice topped with the garnishes of your choice.

Boeuf Stroganoff

Makes Four Very Substantial Portions

This dish is in three parts: you have a bed of rice, you have pieces of tender beef, cooked very quickly in butter, and you have sauce and cream on top. You make the rice ahead of time, you have the sauce ready and keeping hot, and you cook your beef very quickly. Unless you have a very large skillet, it is better to cook the meat in one or two portions and then keep it warm on the rice in the oven. If you put it all in the pan at once it may end up just steaming in its own juices, which is not very good. The taste of the mustard really comes through, so choose a flavorful one you like. The cream we used in the Bistro was English double cream — much thicker than American heavy cream. You may prefer to use crème fraîche or sour cream.

1 cup butter	2 rounded tablespoons tomato paste
2 large onions, minced	4 tablespoons cornstarch
4 cups water	6 tablespoons mustard
1 teaspoon dried mint leaves	Salt and pepper to taste
1 teaspoon dried tarragon leaves	2 pounds very tender cut of beef
5 beef bouillon cubes	4 cups cooked rice
	¼ cup cream, heavy or sour

First make the sauce. Melt 4 tablespoons of butter in a skillet over medium heat and sauté the onions until golden brown. Transfer the onions to a saucepan and add 4 cups water, the mint, tarragon, bouillon cubes, and tomato paste. Bring to a boil, stirring until the cubes dissolve, and allow to simmer for thirty minutes. Mix enough cold water (about ¼ cup) into the cornstarch until it's the consistency of heavy cream. Add to the sauce and allow to bubble for at least two minutes. Add the mustard, stirring in well. Taste for salt and pepper. At this point, you can either cool and refrigerate or freeze the sauce if you're planning ahead. If you do this, reheat before you prepare the meat.

Cut the beef into small strips, about two inches long and between one quarter and one half inch thick. This takes time, but the cooking time is very short - just toss it in the rest of the butter melted in a skillet until it's brown and tender. Remember what I told you about not cooking too much meat at once. If your meat is done and there's still liquid in the skillet, don't throw it out. Add it to the sauce so that taste stays in your dinner.

To serve your boeuf stroganoff, pile rice on each plate. Top with meat. Cover meat with sauce and top that with cream. Any remaining sauce can be served separately for those who like *lots* of sauce.

Pojarsky

I used to do Russian cutlets, but when my mother came back to live in England she had some ideas we tried out and pojarsky was one. It's just the same, pojarsky and cutlets, except pojarsky is veal and cutlets is beef. The shape of these is like an oval patty, so it fits in your gently cupped hand.

You can buy bread crumbs, but I always just put bread in the oven and toast it slowly until it's really dry. Then I put it in the food processor and you've got bread crumbs.

2 onions, minced	1 teaspoon dried tarragon leaves
10 tablespoons butter	2 eggs, beaten
½ cup corn oil	½ teaspoon salt
2 slices bread, crusts removed	½ teaspoon pepper
⅓ cup milk	2 pounds ground veal
1 teaspoon dried mint leaves	2 cups bread crumbs

Sauté the onions in 2 tablespoons butter and 1 tablespoon oil until golden brown and set aside to cool.

Soften the bread slices in the milk, in à large bowl, then squeeze it in your hand until it is soft and smooth. (You don't need the milk anymore.)

When the onions are cool, add them to the bread. Add mint, tarragon, eggs, salt and pepper and mix well. Add the veal and mix thoroughly.

Take a small handful of mixture in one palm. Put a knob of butter in the middle and encase the butter. Roll the pojarsky in bread crumbs and fry in remaining oil until golden brown.

Galubtzy

Serves Eight

1 large cabbage
2 pounds ground beef
Handful white rice, uncooked
1 teaspoon salt
½ teaspoon pepper

2 large onions, minced
1 teaspoon dried mint leaves
1 teaspoon dried tarragon leaves
¼ cup water
6 cups beef stock
Red Sauce (recipe follows)

Cut out the hard stalk of the cabbage. Dunk the head of cabbage into à large pot of boiling water until the outer leaves are softened and you can separate them. Keep dunking and removing leaves until you have a pile of cabbage leaves.

Mix the rest of the ingredients except the stock and sauce together in à large bowl, adding one-quarter cup water to make a smooth mixture.

Take a handful of the mixture and put it in the center of a cabbage leaf. Wrap it neatly and place in à large soup pot. Continue until they are all done. Cover with beef stock and simmer twenty minutes.

To serve, remove the galubtzy with a slotted spoon and ladle on some Red Sauce.

 Red Sauce

Makes about Three Cups

This red sauce and the spaghetti sauce later are very much the same. For this one you add some good Hungarian paprika. For the spaghetti sauce you use Italian herbs and a little bay leaves.

4 tablespoons butter
2 large onions, minced very finely
1 clove garlic, crushed
1 teaspoon dried tarragon leaves, or
  mixed herbs

1 tablespoon paprika
1 small can tomato paste
2 cups beef stock
2 teaspoons cornstarch
¼ cup milk

Melt the butter and sauté the onions in a skillet until they're soft. Transfer to a saucepan. Place over medium heat. Add the garlic, herbs, paprika, tomato paste, and beef stock. Mix well and continue cooking, stirring frequently, for five minutes. Dissolve the cornstarch in the milk and add to the sauce. Let it cook another couple of minutes, stirring constantly.

If you are making this sauce to serve with Galubtzy, you can wait until they are cooked and use the broth in which they were cooked as the stock. You can keep the Galubtzy warm in a covered serving dish in the oven while the sauce cooks.

Crépe á la Reine

Makes Two Servings

This is a very good way to use up the rest of the chicken when you've removed the nice white pieces for Chicken Supreme (see below). You need only three ingredients: cooked chicken pieces, crêpes, and white sauce. I give you the white sauce next, because you need it for Supreme, too.

2 cups cooked chicken, diced

1 batch White Sauce (recipe follows)
4 crêpes (see page 79)

To get it all nice and hot, mix the chicken pieces with one cup of sauce in a saucepan over a low fire, stirring frequently (or you can mix the hot sauce and the chicken and put it in a microwave to heat it through). Put a line of chicken down the middle of a crêpe and roll it up. Serve with more hot white sauce poured over.

White Sauce

Makes about Two Cups

4 tablespoons butter
4 tablespoons all-purpose flour

2 cups boiling chicken stock
Juice of 3 lemons

Melt butter gently so it doesn't brown in a saucepan. Stir in flour, using a nice wooden spoon. Let it bubble a minute or so to cook the flour.

Taste your stock. (If you used the water from poaching a chicken, you may want to make the flavor stronger by adding a chicken bouillon cube.) Add stock slowly to the butter and flour, stirring with a whisk. When it's all mixed, add lemon juice. Start with one lemon and taste as you add more. It's better to have more lemon than less.

Chicken Supreme

This is also just three things together: on a bed of fluffy, hot rice you put a chicken breast and you cover it with White Sauce. The recipe for White Sauce is above. You'll need one batch for four breasts. If you have poached the chicken, then it's easy to remove the skin and take the white meat for the Supreme.

Curry and Rice

Makes Four Cups Sauce

I like curry — but nice, mild curry. In Ceylon they used to cook specially for me. I couldn't eat the regular food, it was so hot. One day we were traveling and a friend said, "Oh, they have lovely buns there." She jumps from the car, goes and buys the lovely buns. There was curry inside. Gosh, it was hot! For hours I could feel that thing burning in my mouth. I don't know how they can eat it.

We used to have on the menu chicken, beef, egg, and kofta curry. They're all the same idea: You take a nice portion of hot rice, you put your chicken, beef, whatever you want on it, and you cover that with good curry sauce.

In London I used to get a curry powder called Venacatchukun, but any kind you can get in the supermarket will work fine, except that you will need to taste and see if the sauce is to your liking — not too mild and not too harsh — and remember next time you make it which kind you used and how much. Here's my sauce.

2 large onions, sliced	1 lemon, diced
2 tablespoons butter	1 cup raisins
2 tablespoons oil	1 teaspoon dried mint leaves
3 cups water	1 teaspoon dried tarragon leaves
2 tablespoons curry powder	½ teaspoon salt
2 cooking apples, diced	¼ teaspoon pepper

Brown the sliced onions in the butter and oil in à large sauté pan. Add a little water to the curry powder to make a thin paste; add it to the onions and mix together. Gradually add the water, mixing constantly until it's a thin sauce. Add all the rest of the ingredients. Bring to a boil and then lower heat to a very slow simmer. Cook until the lemon is soft.

This needs to cook *at least* thirty minutes, but it is much better if you can make it ahead of time. You can cook it slowly all day and it will just get better. The lemon peel especially needs to cook well. You can make it the day before, refrigerate it overnight, and warm it slowly the next day. It smells wonderful.

Pour the sauce over your rice and eggs or meat of choice.

Chicken Curry

I used to take some bigger pieces from my poached chickens. You see, once you have that chicken you can make several different things from it. And if you don't use it today, you keep it in the fridge — it's good tomorrow.

Beef Curry

You could use the same meat you used for Stroganoff, but it's expensive that way. Sometime I used to take beef topside and simmer it — the way we did for the Pojarsky (see page 87) — and then slice it into nice strips for curry.

Egg Curry

This was just a hard-boiled egg, sliced in half and put cut-side down on the rice.

Kofta Curry

Kofta, that means meatballs. The meat mixture we used for the Galubtzy we use for these meatballs. It has a little rice in it. We cook the meatballs gently in hot water, just to cover. Then you get a little stock to use for something else.

Stuffed Green Peppers

Serves Eight

This is just like Galubtzy, so read that recipe, on page 88. Here, you stuff the meat mixture into green peppers instead of rolling it into cabbage leaves.

Slice the tops off of eight medium-sized green bell peppers and remove the seeds and white divider parts inside.

Stuff them — really stuff them — and put the tops back on. Set them in a pot and pour six cups of stock in. Cover the pot.

Bring to a boil and lower the heat to a simmer. Cook twenty minutes.

Serve with the Red Sauce, on page 89, as for Galubtzy.

Vol-au-Vent

Some people want a little different something. I used to buy the pastry cases for the Vol-au-Vent. It's exactly like Crêpe à la Reine (on page 105) only you put the chicken into the little pastry shell instead of into a pancake. Same thing. Pour the White Sauce over and serve. (Vol-au-Vent cases, also called puff pastry shells, are often available fresh at the bakery or in frozen, ready-to-bake form.)

Spaghetti Maison

Makes Eight Servings

Spaghetti is not Russian, but it is good and it is fast. In the Bistro, I said that I did Russian and Continental cooking. Steaks are not Russian; chops are not Russian. You must have something for everybody. Spaghetti is so cheap — I had it for people who couldn't afford more. The Spaghetti Maison was a big plate of spaghetti with just sauce and you put cheese on it — it's a good meal. In the Bistro we cooked the spaghetti in a big pot. We didn't add oil or anything to the water. When the spaghetti was cooked, it was rinsed well in cold water, and then it stayed in the fridge in cold water. It can stay two days like that. When somebody ordered, I would put a good handful into a pot of hot stock we kept always ready on the stove and warm it. At home, I rather heat it in a heavy pan with butter and a shake of salt, stirring and turning it gently with a fork. Then when it's hot, cover and let it sit on a low fire for five minutes, but that was too slow and too expensive for the Bistro.

More important is the sauce, and my sauce is very good. I had spaghetti sauce in lots of places, and I think my sauce is better. It's much more meaty, much more tasty. I keep spaghetti sauce in my freezer if somebody drops in. It should be made in a heavy pot which can be used on top of the stove and then go into the oven. If you don't have one, you'll have to use a big skillet first and then transfer the sauce to a covered dish.

2 onions, minced	1 or 2 bay leaves
2 tablespoons butter	1½ pounds ground beef
2 tablespoons oil	2 small cans tomato paste
1 or 2 cloves garlic	2 beef bouillon cubes
1 teaspoon dried herbs (mixed Italian herbs or half tarragon and half oregano)	2 cups hot water
	½ teaspoon salt
	½ teaspoon pepper

Cook the onions in the butter and oil over medium heat until they are softened, but not browned. Add the garlic, herbs and bay leaves. Add the meat and stir together. Keep stirring until the meat is cooked through — this takes a little patience. Then add the tomato paste. Dissolve the bouillon cubes in two cups of hot water. Start adding the beef bouillon to the meat mixture. Add it gradually, stirring well after each addition. Use your judgment. When it looks the right thickness, add the salt and pepper (add more to your taste if you like), cover the pan and put it in the oven at very low temperature, 250°, for half an hour. Don't throw out the bouillon if you have any left, because you may want to thin the sauce after it has cooked in the oven.

Meatballs

Makes Eight Servings

Use the same recipe as for the filling in Galubtzy on page 88, but don't add rice. Make meatballs whatever size you want. Poach them in just enough beef stock to cover. Make sure they come to a boil before you lower the heat, but don't let them boil much or they'll fall apart! If you've made them about golf-ball size, they'll take about twelve minutes to cook. When they're cooked, put them on some hot spaghetti and pour the sauce over it. Be sure to save the stock they were cooked in. You can use it for something else.

Chops and Entrecôte Garni

Lamb chop, pork chop, *entrecôte* steak — that was just cooked simple. However you like. I used to fry them on top of the stove. Steak garni, lamb chop, pork chop garni — garni, that was with chips and salad. Americans call the chips French fried potatoes, but that's our chips. People wanted chips and salad with steak. Some people would ask for rice with steak. Myself, I like steak and rice. With lamb I always served mint jelly. I don't like the vinegar-base English sauce. Maybe it was good with mutton, but not lamb.

Holstein Steak

I called it that because I put it in bread crumbs, like a schnitzel, with a fried egg on top. It's a nourishing dinner. I take a steak and dip it in beaten egg and then in bread crumbs. Fry it gently. Put maybe a little green pepper on top for decoration — use imagination.

Tournedos Steak

We said "Tournedos if you're lucky" because we would get a whole big beef and cut it up ourselves. We could get sometimes ten, sometimes eighteen filet steaks out of the tenderloin, but when it's gone, that's it. We trimmed off all the fat, wrapped it in bacon and tied it around with a string. Other people put mushrooms, sauces — I don't like that. On the plate was just tournedo, chips, and salad. That's all.

தை

That was all the main things on the menu, except for the sweets. You can see how we did it. But I'll give you some other recipes I used to cook; things people liked, that I used to cook — but not for the Bistro.

Old Fashioned Veal Blanquette

If people wonder what to do with the egg whites they have left over from this recipe, I would tell them to do what my mother used to do. First make a good chicken soup. When it's ready to eat, you keep it on the fire and you stir it slowly. At the same time you dribble the egg whites into the soup. The egg whites make something almost like noodles. The Chinese always have this soup.

2 pounds meaty veal ribs
2 onions
2 carrots, sliced
½ head garlic
Pinch each tarragon, thyme, parsley

2 cubes chicken bouillon
3 tablespoons butter
2 tablespoons flour
1 cup heavy cream
2 egg yolks, beaten
Rice or boiled potatoes, for serving

Place veal in à large pot. Add the onions, carrots, garlic, herbs, and the two bouillon cubes. Cover with water. Simmer until meat is tender. Test by poking with a fork at one and a half hours. It may take two hours if your piece is thick.

Remove the veal from the stock. Keep it warm while making the sauce.

Strain the stock.

Melt the butter in à large saucepan over medium heat; add flour and stir until smooth. Add the cream and stir smooth. Remove from heat and add egg yolks. Return to heat and add the veal stock gradually, stirring constantly, until it is the desired thickness. Put the meat into the sauce. The blanquette is now ready. You can serve it with rice or with boiled potatoes. It is your choice.

Baked Mackerel

Makes Six Servings

This will work well with any firm-fleshed fish.

4 tablespoons butter
1½ pounds mackerel filets
3 large onions, sliced in rings
2 tablespoons corn oil
1 pound tomatoes, sliced

4 cloves garlic, minced
1 teaspoon dried rosemary
1 teaspoon dried basil
¼ cup chopped parsley
1½ teaspoon salt
½ teaspoon pepper

Grease à large baking dish generously with about half the butter. Arrange the fish in it.

Fry the onions until golden brown in the remaining butter and the oil. Add to the onion the tomatoes, garlic, and herbs, including the parsley, and cook together five minutes, turning gently.

Spread this mixture evenly over the fish. Add salt and pepper and bake in 325° oven for one half-hour. You can eat this hot or cold.

Rabbit á la Sylvie

Sylvie is my cousin Valya's wife. She is a very good cook. I used to use her recipe to make rabbit.

2 big onions, sliced
2 tablespoons butter
1 rabbit
1 teaspoon dried tarragon leaves
¼ cup chopped parsley
2 or 3 bay leaves

1½ teaspoon salt
¼ teaspoon pepper
¼ cup cognac
1¼ cup red wine
5 cups water
1 pound mushrooms, sliced

Brown the onions in butter in à large skillet until they are golden. Cut the rabbit into quarters and add it and all the herbs, bay leaves and salt and pepper to the onions. Add cognac, wine, and water. Bring to a boil; lower the heat and let this simmer for half an hour. Slice the mushrooms and add them. Continue simmering until the rabbit is tender, about another half hour.

Serve with boiled potatoes and French beans, or any green vegetable. Now you can eat it and good appetite!

There are two other recipes I would make for people that I couldn't do in the Bistro. I give them to you here anyway.

Aubergine

Makes Four Servings

This is simple to make, but you have to be careful when you are frying it or it burns and it can't sit too long once it's cooked.

1 medium eggplant
2 eggs, beaten

1 cup bread crumbs
3 tablespoons butter
3 tablespoons oil

Trim the ends off the eggplant and slice it in half lengthwise. Then slice into half-round slices, about one half inch thick. Dip in the eggs and coat in bread crumbs. Melt the butter with the oil in a skillet over fairly high fire. Add the breaded eggplant slices and fry until golden brown, turning once during the cooking.

Fruit Pilaf

Makes Eight Servings

This is a very tasty dish. It is sweet and goes well with roast chicken, or you can put pieces of chicken in it, but many times I would serve it when I was having hors d'oeuvres first. Then I would just serve the pilaf and a salad and then a sweet. It can be a very satisfying meal like that. Everybody was happy.

1½ cups rice
¼ cup brown sugar
1 good tablespoon honey

¼ pound butter, melted
6 ounces dried fruit, plumped (raisins, prunes, apricots, or a mixture of all three)

Put the rice on to cook first. You can make the rice ahead of time, or use leftover rice which you have warmed up by putting it in a baking dish, dotting it with butter, covering it, and putting it in a 300° oven to warm while you make the fruit.

Use a baking dish that has a cover. Add the sugar and honey to the butter and mix well. Dump in the fruit and stir until it is all coated. Add one vodka glass of water — that's about 1 tablespoon. Cover and put in oven at 300° for twenty minutes. To serve, put the fruit on top of the rice. Drizzle the juice from the fruit over the rice.

SWEETS

We didn't have much sweets at the Bistro. Mostly it was things we could fix quickly, or things where I could buy the ingredients made already and put them together. There was the trifle, the custard, my *cernic*, and the orange salad.

The other sweets were all vanilla ice cream with something else: meringue glacé was a meringue with ice cream in the middle, fruit melba was ice cream and banana or tinned fruit with sauce on top. The sauce was just jam made a little thinner with hot water. For my chocolate sauce I used to buy Cadbury's chocolate, melt it over hot water, and serve it warm. It's very easy.

Of course when I cooked at home, I used to do other things, too. Although we never used to have much sweets in my home when I was growing up that I remember, I like to try to make new things. So later I give you my recipe for chocolate mousse, too.

ぷ

Trifle

Of course it was England, so we had trifle. That's very English. It's also very easy.

Plain cake, cut in small cubes (you can use loaf cake, plain white or yellow cake, sponge cake, even pound cake)
Strawberry jam

Fruit
3 cups custard (recipe follows)
Cream (optional)
Sherry (if you're at home)

This is another one of my fiddle recipes. You use what you have.

You make a big bowl of this and keep it in the fridge and serve portions.

Start with à layer of jam you have thinned with water so it's liquidy.

Then you put à layer of cake. Plain cake you can get anywhere in England or America. It goes in nicely. Then put a little bit more thicker jam, then you cover with cake again.

Then I used to use some nice fruit: any kind you had in cans — peaches, pears, apricot. Then you put custard (see below). In England you buy custard sauce in packages and mix it up, but you can make your own. It's not difficult. You can put cream on the trifle or not.

When I make it at home, of course I sprinkle sherry on the cake layers, too, but in the Bistro I didn't have a license and if you don't have a license and you sell anything with alcohol you're against the law. My favorite customers, I used to put on a little sherry. Then I had too many favorite customers. I had to stop.

Custard Sauce   **Makes Three Cups**

5 egg yolks
⅔ cup sugar
⅓ cup all-purpose flour

¼ teaspoon salt
1½ cups milk
½ cup cream
1½ teaspoons vanilla extract

Beat egg yolks in a medium-sized bowl. Combine sugar, flour, and salt and beat into the egg yolks. Combine milk and cream in a heavy saucepan and heat to just below boiling. Add to the egg mixture, beating all the time. Put this back into the sauce pan. Cook over low heat, stirring constantly, until it is thick and smooth. Remove from heat and stir in vanilla extract. Allow to cool to room temperature before making the trifle.

Luba's Special Cernic

Makes Twelve to Twenty Cernic

These are pancakes and cheese filling. You can make them folded over, like the piroshky. You can stuff them like crêpes. You can spread the cheese filling onto a pancake and roll it into a tube. Or you can make a sandwich with a pancake, cheese filling, and another pancake on top. They go very well after a light summer dinner when you are still hungry.

½ cup raisins, plumped in water or
    brandy
4 egg yolks
¼ cup sugar

1½ pounds cream cheese
¼ cup heavy cream, to thin the filling if
    it stands overnight
One batch crêpes (see page 79)

You can plump the raisins two ways: you can put them in boiling water and let them boil for two minutes, then let them cool; or you can let them sit overnight in brandy. In either case you must drain them very well so they don't make the cheese filling too soft and runny.

Combine egg yolks and sugar in a food processor or mixer. Let them whirl a few minutes because you must not have that granulate texture. Add the cheese and mix well. Mix in the raisins by hand.

The filling can be made ahead of time. It can stay in the fridge four or five days. It doesn't go sour, but it does get thicker and thicker. When you plan to use it, thin it to desired consistency with heavy cream.

How many cernic you have depends on how much filling you use. Just dollop it on a pancake as you like.

Orange Salad

This was not what some people call salad. It was oranges sliced thin, arranged in a dish, and then orange juice squeezed over. You let it sit a couple of hours in the fridge and it is very tasty and refreshing. It doesn't need anything else added.

Chocolate Mousse   **Makes Six Servings**

My mousse is excellent the day it is made. The next day it settles down a little. Then it is denser and even more chocolate tasting.

18 ounces semisweet or bittersweet chocolate   12 eggs, separated, at room temperature

Melt chocolate in a double boiler over hot water. Cool it.

Beat egg whites until firm. Transfer to à large bowl.

Beat the egg yolks (you can use the bowl you just beat the egg whites in) until they are light yellow.

Add the cooled chocolate to the egg yolks and beat both together.

Fold the chocolate into the egg whites. Put into refrigerator for two hours to set.

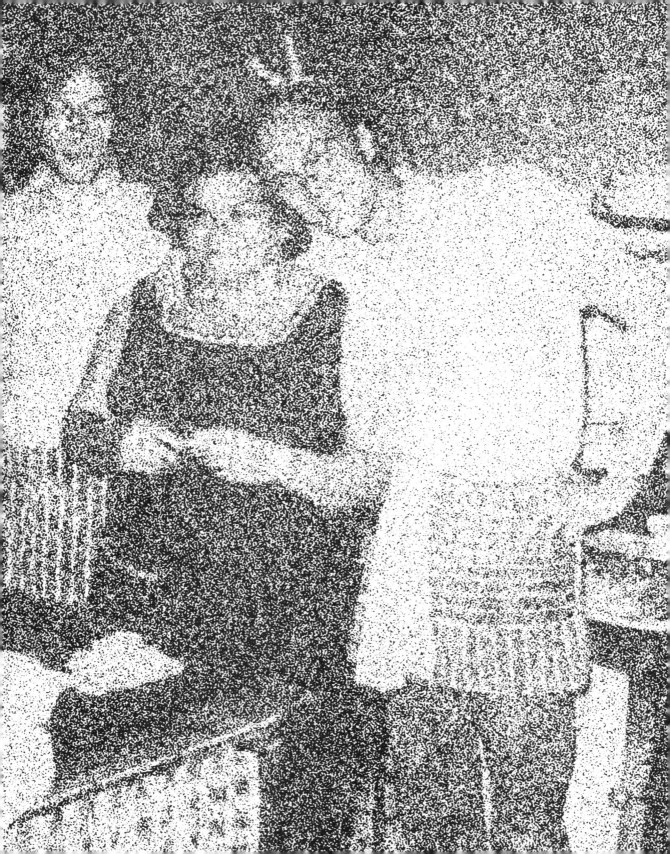